Half a Slice
of Bread

Half a Slice of Bread

CAUGHT IN THE CURRENTS OF
WAR, A FAMILY JOURNAL

Ieva Neimanas Pipyne

ISBN: 1522792899
ISBN 13: 9781522792895

Contents

Introduction

THIS IS THE STORY OF my family, who were caught up in the political and military events of World War II from 1941 to 1950. Our normal life in a small town in northern Lithuania ended with the invasion of our homeland by Nazi Germany, followed by the Soviet occupation. I lived through these events as a young child.

I have thought about this turbulent period of our lives. I am aware that millions of people suffered and were uprooted, and millions lost their lives during this period. I am not a holocaust survivor. However, I have found that little has been written and little is known about the life of the people considered ethnic Germans (Volksdeutsche) by the Nazi regime, who left their homeland to escape the Soviet-Communist occupation. Many decided to leave for Nazi Germany, not because they considered themselves German or were supporters of Hitler's policies, but because of fear and knowledge of the Soviet regime.

There are gaps in my story, and memories of the events have lost their sharp edges over the years. My parents and older relatives have died, and I have lost their recollections and explanations. There remain only two family members—my brother, Stasys, and my second cousin Renate (Barnelis) Sanner—who lived through that turbulent war period and have helped to reconstruct our experiences.

I have asked myself why I failed to ask my parents to fill in the gaps in my recollections and explain what I could not understand or remember about this confusing time. During the actual events, it was unwise and also dangerous to ask too many questions. There was little privacy, and someone might overhear you questioning the authorities and report you. Some situations and events moved so quickly that there was no time to formulate questions. All we could do was adapt to constantly changing circumstances.

Once we arrived in the United States in 1950, we scrambled to make a living, adjust to a different way of life, and learn a new language. When we were somewhat settled, there was a desire to just live and let go of the past. But the past stayed with all of us.

Family and Home

My parents were Kazimira (Rimkeviciute) Neimanas and Stasys Neimanas. My mother was born in 1901 Latvia, where her father was working for the railroad. She had only one brother, Jonas (John), who was two years older. My father was born in Lithuania in 1899, the youngest of ten siblings.

Both my parents were displaced from their homes to Russia during the First World War and returned to Lithuania after 1918, when the country regained its independence. My parents met while both were working at an estate. My mother, Kazimira, was a reserved, black-haired, beautiful woman with a glimmer of a smile on her face, and worked as a secretary. My father, Stasys, a sociable and approachable person who loved life, was the estate manager. They were married in 1928. Their firstborn, daughter Jadviga, died in her first year of life of unknown causes. Daughter Margarita was born May1930; son Stasys, was born September 1932; and I, Ieva, was born September 1934. My youngest brother, John (Jonas), was born May 1940 when the turmoil was already brewing in Eastern Europe, including in Lithuania.

Our Neimanas family lived in a small town in Lithuania called Nemunelio-Radviliskis, located at the junction of two rivers. The household consisted of our immediate family; our maternal grandfather; our nanny, Ane; and Adele, our household help. A seamstress came to live with us for a period of time every spring and fall. She sewed new clothing for the family members, since no ready-made clothes were available.

Our home was on the northern border of Lithuania and Latvia, on the high bank where the Apascia River met the Nemunelis River. Our father, an ordained minister of the Evangelical Reformed Church, was the pastor of the Protestant congregation. The church sat across the street from our home. Both the church and the churchyard, also on the high bank of the Nemunelis River, were as much home to us as our orchard was.

Our family owned some land and had cows, pigs, sheep, horses, chickens, ducks, and a dog. Aside from our home, there was a barn, a horse stable, a chicken coop, and a dugout cellar, where potatoes, carrots, beets, and other produce, as well as ice cut from the river, were stored. On hot summer days and for special occasions, my mother treated us to homemade ice cream, using ice from the cellar. The whole family participated in cranking the handle of the ice-cream "machine" for this delicious cold treat.

Electricity had not yet reached the small towns, so we used kerosene lamps and candles for lighting. Water came from an outdoor well, using a winding crank. We baked our own bread, and nanny Ane and my mother spun our wool on a spinning wheel in our huge kitchen. In winter, we set up a loom in the kitchen, and our mother, nanny Ane, and Adele wove woolen and linen cloth for us. We traveled by horse and wagon or carriage in the summer and by sled in the winter.

My home town, Nemunelio-Radviliskis, on the bank of Apascia River.1938

Nemunelis River in spring with the Lithuanian Evangelical
Reformed Church on the high bank

Our family home in N.-Radviliskis, circ.1931/32

. Our family in 1935/36 with maternal grandfather. Brother,
Stasys and I are standing on birch stumps.

Sister Rita and brother Stasys standing by gate that leads to a field, 1934

Our extended family, 1933. Left to right, back rowe: cousin, Danute Kregzde, nanny
Ane holding brother, Stasyss and father's cousin Elzbute. Middle rowe: aunt Ona
Ycas holding daughter, Onyte, my paternal grandmother, and my parents. Sister,
Rita has bows in her hair. On ground: aunt Ona's sons, Adolis, Martinas and Jonas

Leaving Home

ORDINARY LIFE CAME TO AN end sometime in 1940. Soon after John's birth, the United Soviet Socialist Republic (USSR) invaded Lithuania. The Communist Party placed a young couple, who we did not know, to live in our home. They were trusted Communist Party members. Their job was to keep an eye on us, especially our father, and our activities. Communism did not believe in private property, and, therefore, our home was no longer ours. We were considered "bourgeoisie" and a threat to communism.

We were suspect because of our father's education and position, as well as for his previous activities dating from WWI and the overthrow of the Russian czar. My father had supported the czarist side and opposed communism. He was captured, and, as a prisoner of the Bolsheviks in Siberia, cleared the Siberian railroad in winter so that trains could go through. His experiences from that war and his captivity left him terrified of communism.

Already Lithuanians were being arrested, incarcerated, executed, and deported to labor camps in Soviet Russia and Siberia. Our family was clearly marked and suspect. Our aunt Fele's husband was arrested during the first weeks of occupation and executed. Aunt Fele was never able to accept this; she continued to write letters to the Soviet government asking for an accounting of his fate.

At this time, there was still a nonaggression pact between Russia and Germany, and the Lithuanians with demonstrated German ancestry could immigrate to Germany as "Volksdeutsche." Our parents had to choose whether to remain in occupied Lithuania and accept deportation to Siberia as a good outcome or to leave for Germany, where the living conditions and our fate were unknown. They decided that we had a better chance of survival if we left for Germany.

I was six years old in February 1941 when we packed up all the permissible essentials, under the watchful eyes of the communist couple, and started into the unknown. Most of our relatives had made the same choice, risking life in Germany rather than remaining in occupied Lithuania. Our maternal grandfather chose to stay in Lithuania, as did one of my father's sisters Aunt Helce, my godmother. Danute (Ycas) Kregzde, my father's niece, who was a dentist, remained in Kaunas, Lithuania. My mother's brother, Stasys, and his family decided to remain in occupied Lithuania as well.

It was bitterly cold in early February 1941 when our family set off in a sleigh from Nemunelio-Radviliskis for Birzai, where we boarded a train. Nanny Ane came with our family, carrying Johnny, just a bundle, in her arms. More of our relatives, friends, and strangers joined us on this exodus. We tried to stay close to our relatives: the Barnelis family, the Ycas family, our aunt Fele, and great-aunt Lisa Greenwelt. There was a sense of comfort in being with relatives and friends.

Our father's niece Onyte Ycas wrote a letter dated March 5, 1941, to her friend Jurate Margaviciene, who remained in Lithuania, describing our journey from Birzai to Utrata, our first transition-and-screening camp. For some reason, the letter was never mailed. Here is a translated summary of this letter.

You probably expected a letter from Rostock (Germany), but it will arrive from Lodz (Poland). Let me tell you from the beginning. As you know, we left Birzai at nine thirty in the morning and arrived in Panavezis around one in the afternoon, where we stayed overnight. We spent about three hours in the train station, while our luggage was examined by the border patrol. We got very cold, and cousin Renate fell in a puddle while running to her father. The train finally started up around four o'clock. Not all our family members were assigned to the same train car. We rode for a long time. We bedded down in our compartments, for there was nothing else to do.

In the morning, we crossed the border and stopped in Lauksargius (Memel), where we got to freshen up, had breakfast, and heard our first speech.

Then we traveled a whole day and night again. During the night, we rode through Danzig and crossed the Visla River. It is too bad that I could not see anything, because the shades were drawn to prevent air attacks. So we rode all night not seeing where we were going. In the morning, when the shades were lifted, we saw plains everywhere, but we had been expecting mountains. It dawned on us that we were in Poland. It turns out that the rail tracks to Rostock were jammed with trains, and so we had to go to Lodz. We rode through many Polish cities and saw bombed-out homes. We rode as far as Pabianicos, Poland. From there, we were taken by buses to a factory. Here we had to take showers, and our clothing was disinfected. Our hair was examined for lice. It was nice to have a shower, and then get warm clothing. We also got something to eat and went to sleep. So our journey took three days and three nights. The next day we had to sign up with whom we were going to live and then taken to camp.

Onyte never had a chance to mail this letter, and it stayed with her for about fifty years before she gave a copy to her niece Renate (Barnelis) Sanner. When Renate learned that I was interested in writing our family's story, she gave me a copy of this letter.

Introduction to the Third Reich

I DO NOT REMEMBER HOW long we stayed in Utrata, Poland, and how we left for Teodoris, nor how long we were in either transition camp. What I do remember about this last transition camp is that armed German soldiers were watching our father, Renate's father, and other adult men digging latrines—simple ditches with raised saplings on which to perch to relieve ourselves. The soldiers laughed and pointed at the men. I felt angry at the soldiers for ridiculing my father. I also felt humiliated, exposed, and afraid that I might fall into the trough. How much more difficult and degrading it must have been for my parents.

It was in this town that we first saw men wearing lightweight, striped clothing that looked like pajamas, working under armed guards, and we realized they were Jews. It was also in this town that all of us were taken to a movie theater to see a German propaganda film, *The Eternal Jew*. Our indoctrination had begun.

We arrived in Wangerin, Prussia, (currently Wegorzyno, Poland) by train on a cold and wet day. It was evening and raining as we walked through the gates of this fenced-in "Auslander Lager" (foreigner camp). The clay clung to our shoes, and it was difficult to walk while carrying our meager belongings. We were marched into our assigned wooden barracks and into a designated room. Luckily, we got a room for just our family of seven; smaller families had to share rooms. There were three bunk beds with straw mattresses, a table, some wooden stools, one window, a bare light bulb hanging from the ceiling, and a small coal/coke burning stove.

In the morning, as we looked out the window, we saw that the barracks stood in a field and were surrounded by a barbed-wire fence. There were many barracks, about thirty. They were all alike; a hallway ran through the middle, and identical rooms, at least ten, were on each side. There was a door on both ends and a common bathroom at the front with several flush toilets and several sinks and showers. The barracks were built from raw, unfinished wood without insulation. The camp was bare and raw, with no vegetation in sight, barracks lined up one next to another. The focal point was the central parade ground with a flying German flag.

Each morning, all camp residents gathered on the parade ground, saluted the flag with arms raised, sang "Die Fahne Hoch," the SA (Sturm Abteilung) party anthem, and "Deutschland, Deutschland Uber Alles," the Nazi German national anthem, and shouted, "Heil Hitler," at the end. The camp commandant gave a speech and strict orders that we were all expected to obey. Our aunt Fele was the translator, because most of us did not speak German. We and our parents, the adults, were no longer free people. The gate to Wangerin's "Auslander Lager" was guarded by armed soldiers, and we were captives.

Our lives were under complete control of the Third Reich's German Lager Fuehrer, who wore highly polished knee-high boots, carried a short whip, and always walked with a dog. German news was broadcast by a loudspeaker. Food was prepared in a common kitchen. Adult women had to work in the kitchen, peeling potatoes, scrubbing pots and pans—whatever was needed. A family member had to stand in line every day, for every meal, in the community building to pick up our allotted portion. Breakfast consisted of artificial coffee (Ersatz Kaffee) that was made from grains, chicory, or even roasted oak seeds, a slice of bread, and some jam. Lunch was a thin gruel, and dinner was two slices of bread with sausage and peppermint tea to drink. Children under six years of age got some milk and mashed potatoes.

Adult men were "recruited" to serve in the army and were sent to the Eastern Front. Of course, they were always considered volunteers. Initially the Germans were selective. They wanted their soldiers to be a certain height, blond, and blue-eyed. As the war progressed and casualties mounted, the standards for induction "volunteers" were revised.

There were daily inspections of all barracks and rooms to check that the beds were made to specifications and that everything was in order. We had to stand and salute the inspecting guards and remain standing until they left. On Sundays, we, the camp detainees, were given a special treat: holding hands, under guard supervision, we were led for a walk down a paved highway, like small children through the forest. We had to sing German folksongs, like "Kommt ein Vogel geflogen." Maybe this was a way to enhance our German language and make us feel more patriotic.

School-aged children had to attend school. Initially our schooling was in the camp itself. Not only did we have to cope with a brand new language, but we also had to learn to write the gothic lettering. To our relief, the next year Germany adopted Latin lettering. Later we attended German schools in town. We left for school in groups and returned in groups. Corporal punishment was used for many misdeeds, such as spilling ink. The culprit had to stand in front of the classroom and hold out a hand that the teacher hit with a stick.

It was in this bleak and inhospitable environment that our brother Johnny developed pneumonia. Antibiotics had not been discovered yet; nutrition was sparse, medical care questionable. I thought it was a miracle that Johnny lived, but, in reality, it was nanny Ane's care and devotion to him and our family that saved his life. She had seen many hardships growing up but had become a nurturing, calming member of our family.

Soon after our arrival at Wangerin's foreigner's camp, all the hundreds of thousands of us had to submit to a physical examination. A special train had pulled up close to our camp, and residents were marched to the train. We had to undress and go naked from one train car to the next, where a different procedure was performed. What stands out in my mind was the car where blood samples were taken from our earlobes to determine our blood types. Then our blood-group types were tattooed into our under-arm. I screamed and fought the procedure and was slapped by the doctor. What was the purpose of doing blood typing on all of us? It was a humili-ating, degrading experience that a six-year-old found scary. The adults were wise and knew not to grumble or protest. We were no longer in charge of our lives.

Over time, things eased up, and people were permitted to leave camp and go into town or on walks. Going mushroom hunting with my mother and bringing back beautiful, delicious boletus was a refreshing adventure. We gathered the berries that we found and occasionally got some fruit from local farmers who saw our plight. It was forbidden to beg, but, at times, my brother Stasys and I sneaked out of the camp through the bottom of the fence and begged from farmers in the area. Food was scarce, and any extra edible was a treat, even a potato on bread sprinkled with stolen onions from the kitchen. One morning when nanny Ane found a drowned mouse in the milk container, we drank the milk in spite of the mouse.

Sometime during our stay in Wangerin, war prisoners were brought into our camp. They were pitiful: emaciated, with torn, scant clothing, many wearing heavy wooden clogs, some barefoot. They were herded toward the back of the camp and had to sleep outside on bare ground under armed guards. During the day, they were marched outside the fence to dig trenches around the camp. Our barrack was next to the fence, and we could watch them through our window. It was forbidden to approach them or speak to them. When they thought the guards were not watching, they occasionally tried to sneak into the farmer's field, where turnips for cattle feed grew. If they were spotted, they were beaten, or all were made to run uphill along the fence. Many stumbled and fell, and then they were kicked or hit with the butts of the guards' guns. When their day's work was done, they were marched into the camp again. They had to go past the communal kitchen where trash barrels with kitchen waste such as potato peelings and rancid meat scraps were left. They broke out of the ranks and grabbed whatever they could.

One day, my mother gave me a half slice of bread to sneak through the fence to the starving prisoners. I took along a cloth to shake out the crumbs so that I could hide my action. I got close to the fence and snuck the bread out through the loops. The men pounced on it on their knees, pushing and shoving one another, hands grabbing and fighting for a small half slice of bread. I started screaming, "You are animals, just like they—" Nanny Ane rushed up to me, slapped me, and pulled me away into the barrack and our room. We all sat there, not speaking, waiting and listening for boot steps and guards to open the door. Our luck held out; I had not been seen or heard.

Fear was always present. Renate's sister, Erika got sick with a rash and a cough. The family knew the morning room inspection was coming, and all sick children were taken to the camp hospital. Her parents hid her in one of the beds and told her to be still and quiet. Then the family waited and prayed that Erika would not be noticed and taken away. They were lucky; Erika stayed quiet as a mouse.

I don't know for exactly how many years we lived in Wangerin, but we celebrated at least several Christmases in this camp. All the residents had to go to the camp mess room, where we sat at long tables and listened to the camp commandant and other uniformed officials give long propaganda speeches. Very young children got an orange as a gift. John was one of them. He remembered this and related that he wondered what the orange thing was. Was it for bouncing and playing? What was it? There was a large Christmas tree in the hall and we all had to sing, "O Tannenbaum."

In the first year that we were in Wangerin, a mastoid infection reoccurred in my left ear. After being examined in the camp infirmary, I was sent to a hospital in Stargard (currently Szczencinski, Poland). My father was permitted to accompany me by train. Once I was admitted, he had to leave. Initially, I was very sick and do not remember all that happened, aside from a repeat surgery. As I was beginning to recover, I remember standing in a child's crib with tall side rails. There were other beds and children in the room, but I did not speak or understand German yet and was very frightened.

One day, two nurses came to my bed, lifted me up, and carried me to a small room. I knew immediately that this was not an examining room, as it only had a table and a built-in bench around the table. The nurses put me down on the seat, spoke to me, and left. It seemed to me that I was there for a long time.

I wondered what would happen to me. I had already heard that Germans were doing medical experiments. I was frightened and started crying. Finally the door opened, and the two nurses came in with a cake with candles on it. Then I really started crying. It was my seventh birthday, and they wanted it to be special for me, but I had suspected the worst. I was crying out of guilt and relief. A few minutes later, my dad walked in. He had special permission to visit me. He picked me up in his arms and held me. I felt safe. He brought me a small silver tumbler with a few bachelor buttons in it. I still have it. This little tumbler is filled with a multitude of feelings and memories. The fear in strange surroundings, guilt for misunderstanding the nurses' intentions, and the joy and relief I felt in my father's arms.

Not all times were bad; there were also good times. Our aunt Ona Ycas, our father's sister and her family lived in the same barrack as our family. Some evenings, we visited in their room, played cards and talked. We played gin rummy, a game called one thousand, and many others. Sometimes our mother told our fortunes by reading the cards. In good weather, we children played in the back of the barracks where there was a bit of grass. We did not have any toys but invented games with sticks, made our own clay balls, and played a version of jacks. Sister Rita was a master at this game. Our parents also helped us make our own ball out of fabric and stuffed with I don't know what. We invented all kinds of games. My favorite pastime was listening to our father tell us about his experiences in WWI.

Some time during our stay in Wangerin, our father left and was sent to Occupied USSR, because he was fluent in the Russian language. This was hard on Mom, and I remember her crying for days. Her fears and worries must have been greatly increased by the repeated screenings (interrogations) she had to endure during our stay in Wangerin. She was suspected of being not Lithuanian, but Polish, because of her maiden name and because she had been baptized a Catholic. This meant that our family was not eligible for resettlement and return to Lithuania.

There was always a threat of being sent to a concentration camp at the morning "Appels" muster. We did not know precisely what was happening in concentration camps, but stories leaked out about brutality, starvation, and systematic killings in these camps. Wangerin was designated an "A Lager," which meant we were not eligible to return to our homelands, because our loyalty (Germanization) was not established.

Our family in our room in camp for foreigners, Wangerin, showing 2 bunk beds.
All photos from Wangerin, were taken by cousin Adolis, with a
Retina camera, that he had brought from Lithuania, 1941/42

Our family in camp Wangerin, by window and smoke pipe of
our room with home-made ball by brother, Stasys feet,

Earliest closeup photo of brother, Johnny and brother, Stasys, 1941

My photo with view of our barrack in 1941/42

Celebrating Christmas 1942 in aunt, Ona's room. Back row:Cousin Martinas, nanny Ane, and aunt, Ona. Middle row: brother, Stasys, aunt, Fele, and cousin, Onyte. Front row: mother holding sister, Rita brother, Johnny, and I.

Summer 1942/43 outside of barbed wire fenced in camp of Wangerin. Our father is already someplace in Russia

Group of children at front door of our barrack. Cousin, Erika Barnelis is in front rowe at the right side. I am standing behind her. Brother, Johnny is front center. Winter, 1941/42.

Another group of children from our barrack, sister, Rita is on right side, leaning against door frame; cousin, Onyte is the tallest on left side leaning against door.

Upgrading Our Status as "Germanized"

OUR FAMILY WAS TRANSFERRED TO an "Auslander Lager" in Koslin (currently Koszalin, Poland) in the late summer of 1943. I was not quite nine years old. This was a much larger camp with more barracks and various nationalities and many Russian speaking people. It was labeled an "O Lager," which meant we were eligible and considered trustworthy enough to be resettled in Lithuania. I don't know what brought about our improved status; I think that it was our father's service in Russia. Our life in this camp was considerably freer. There were no more daily room inspections or daily flag-raising routines. There was no barbed-wire fence or trench around the camp, and the guards at the gate were no longer armed. But our life still depended completely on the camp administration. We had to stand in line to receive our allocated food rations on a daily basis as well as our coal ration for the little burner in our rooms. But we were free to leave the camp without special permits. School-aged children attended public German schools in town. Sister Rita had to take a train to the school she was attending. Stasys and I also used public transportation to attend separate schools in town.

The school I attended was just about in the town center. It was a two-story brick building with an enclosed school yard. Recess was a sad and lonely time for me. I cannot remember the other children doing anything mean to me, but they all played together, with much chattering and laughter, while I stood by the wall, all by myself. When we returned to the classroom after one recess, we had a math test. I finished it quickly and handed my paper in to the teacher at the head of the classroom. As I sat down, I suddenly started crying. The teacher looked at me and said, "*Du hast Heimweh*. You are homesick." I felt that this teacher understood what I was feeling.

This teacher befriended me and wanted to know about our family and our life. I think she wanted to help us in some way. She requested that our nanny Ane come with me to her home to help with preserving fruit for the winter. Nanny Ane and I went to her home. This was the first time since we had left Lithuania in 1941 that I had been in a home that had furniture, curtains, and dishes. While nanny Ane worked in the kitchen, the teacher gave me books to read and let me wander through her home. It seemed beautiful and grand to me. Then her brother came into the room where I was reading. He had a SA (Sturm Abteilung) uniform and highly polished knee boots. He did not say anything to me, but my heart froze. I was scared. I could hardly wait for nanny Ane to finish with her work. I wanted to go home to the miserable camp where I understood the rules. Finally, nanny Ane finished, and we got to take some fruit preserves and potatoes with us.

Later, when we were leaving for Lithuania, this teacher gave me a book as a remembrance. I lost the book and forgot this teacher's name. She showed me understanding and kindness and tried to be helpful to our family. I wish I could honor her memory by at least remembering her name. (Maybe her name was Fraulein Kasten?)

In this camp, what was watched carefully and reinforced by written signs, verbal reprimands, and indoctrination, was, "*Wir mussen immer nur deutsch sprechen*. We must speak only German." Brother Stasys was once punished for speaking Lithuanian and had to write, "*Ich werde immer nur deutsch sprechen,*" five hundred times. There were also organized events for all residents, where we gathered in large halls and listened to speeches, watched propaganda films, and listened to Hitler's filmed speeches. We frequently saw weekly news films about the progress of the war that portrayed great victories of the Third Reich or "strategic withdrawals." It was also during this time, that we saw and heard multitudes of bombers flying east, but we did not know their nationalities. Were these Nazi planes flying to bomb the Soviet front, or were these Allied planes on a mission to halt German advancement?

The war's impact on the economy affected our basic needs. Food allocations decreased and being semi hungry was a normal feeling. We were happy that our dad was able to send us food packages from Russia, which we awaited eagerly. We stood around with mounting anticipation while Mom opened the package. It was like Christmas. The box was usually made of wood and lined with various improvised packaging materials—at times shredded newspaper, straw, moss, or anything else our dad could think of. There would be flour; a chunk of bacon at times; sometimes eggs, usually at least a few broken, making a sticky mess; and, almost always, dried blueberries. These were our snacks, our candy, our chips.

The allocated coal and coke rations shrank drastically, and our room was cold. We were all warned about the dire consequences of stealing even a couple coal chunks.

Our camp was on the outskirts of town. On the other side, there was a big field with a small airport and what we guessed were antiaircraft installations. Behind this field, there was a forest where, several times a week, we foraged for pinecones and dried twigs. Both Stasys and I remember this well. I went most frequently with nanny Ane. We tied up the twigs in bundles with twine from packages sent by Papa, hoisted them on our backs, and carried them home. Nothing was wasted, because everything was in short supply.

Our clothing and shoes were wearing out. Clothing was passed on from "bigger to smaller." Seams were taken out of coats, trousers, and dresses. The pieces were re-cut and recombined to make them into something wearable. We also started receiving used clothing and shoes. We didn't know where the donations came from. Then stories were whispered that these items were confiscated property from political prisoners and Jews who had been sent to concentration camps. Stories spread that precious stones and other valuable items could be found in the clothing. I don't know of anyone who found anything, but I believe these stories were based on actual attempts by some concentration-camp prisoners to survive and to have something valuable to barter with for a slice of bread for their lives.

In this camp, I have the first clear recollection of my brother Johnny. I was playing in the big communal sandbox with him. It was next to the kindergarten building, where even school-aged children gathered in the late afternoon for snacks. We held hands and, instead of a prayer, recited in chorus, *"Mein Magen ist leer und brummt wie ein Beer.* My stomach is empty and growls like a bear." Life was pretty bleak for all of us. This was 1944, and all our relatives and friends were scattered, living in other camps or returned to Lithuania. We greatly missed our father and the sense of comfort we felt when he was with us.

Going Home

FINALLY IN SPRING 1944, OUR family got permission to return to Lithuania. I don't know why or how or who made the decision, but we were elated, just thinking that we would be going home. My next memory is from when we were already in Lithuania, traveling in a freight car with many strangers who spoke Lithuanian. It was a casual, relaxed conversation that included my mother, nanny Ane, and others travelers. We sat on our bundles of belongings. I sat next to my mother. I turned to her and said, *"Mutti,"* and the wagon fell silent. I had committed a terrible blunder. We were seen as German collaborators, spies. Just one word, "Mommy," uttered in German changed the relationship between our family and the Lithuanians who had not fled their homeland in 1941. Our family knew we were not welcome back in our native country, which we had missed and longed to return to. The rest of the journey is wiped from my memory.

We did not return to our home in Nemunelio-Radviliskis, since it had become the property of the State when it was invaded by the Soviets and put to public use. Instead we were sent to Papilys, Lithuania, a small town where our father was born and where his father had served as a pastor to the Lithuanian Evangelical Reformed community. We were driven to an estate, which in the past had belonged to a French family who had fled Lithuania, either from the Soviet or the German occupation. It was our family's responsibility to manage the estate and meet the German requisition quota of the harvest from this estate.

It was early spring, and buttercups bloomed in the marsh by a pond that was part of the estate. The big main home had hardly any furniture in it but had a grand piano in the living room. Aside from the house, there was a coach house with an old, elegant, covered carriage with glass windows and a driver's seat. We loved playing in it and pretending to go to balls and great receptions. There was also a stable with a horse and barn.

The most fascinating part of this estate was the long drive, bordered by trees that led around a hunting lodge that was surrounded by a water-filled moat. Every tree on this drive had crows' nests, and, since it was spring and hatching time, their cawing was incessant and loud. Many hatchlings fell out of the nests, and, as we approached, the parents dive-bombed us to protect their young. Nonetheless, we loved going to this hunting lodge, which was built like a round castle turret, and we explored, letting our imaginations fly. I felt free.

It was nice to wake up and see grass and plants, to have windows, and to not worry if our neighbors could hear us through the walls. It felt great to have so much space, even without any furniture in the house.

The occupying German administration set the overall plan of what we were to grow and produce. One of our obligations was to raise turkeys. Each morning, nanny Ane and I went out to pick certain wild plants that we chopped, mixed with some type of grain, and fed the turkey chicks. They were free-roaming, and I enjoyed feeding them and seeing them grow. I don't know what other obligations my parents had. I was too busy having a wonderful time.

My father's sister, my godmother, Aunt Helce, came to visit us. I remember walking with her through the wetland and learning about different plants from her. Other visitors to Papilys were the Barnelis family, with whom we left Lithuania in 1941. We were close, not only because of our family relationship, but through our shared experience of the first journey and life in the German camps. Their family consisted of father Fritzas Barnelis, who was a minister and had studied theology at the same university as my father. His wife, Birute, was my father's niece. They had two daughters, Renate and Erika.

The Barnelis family returned to Lithuania some time in 1943. They were assigned the responsibility of cultivating, harvesting, and meeting the requisition quotas of the occupying Nazi administration. This property, called Simpeliskis, had belonged to Birute Barnelis's family in the past. Life was difficult for them, as the quotas were extremely high and difficult to meet. Farm help was not readily available to assist with the planting and harvesting. Young men were drafted into the military, imprisoned, and deported to Siberia, and many of those who remained joined the partisan freedom fighters in the forests.

Initially, only Birute and her daughters, Renate, age eleven, and Erika a six-year-old, were responsible for the oversight of this farm, but because of the partisan threat, it was too dangerous for them to remain there overnight. So each evening, they returned to Birzai. Birute struggled to maintain the farm and meet the quotas for months with the help of only Renate and Erika before her husband, Fritzas returned from the Eastern front. Fritzas, had been drafted into the German military and was unable to help them. Eventually, he was discharged to return and manage the farm. In addition to his management duties, he was responsible for the defense of the farm and the townspeople. There were partisans in this area, and, at times, they came to different farmsteads for food, clothing, or other essentials. Since the Barnelis were Lithuanians who had returned from Germany, they were seen as German collaborators, the enemy, and the partisans could attack them.

While staying at the farm, Erika went to play in the barn and accidently injured herself. Somehow, she caught her chin on a large nail and ripped the flesh up to her lip and was bleeding profusely. Birute set out for Birzai to find a doctor, but could not find one to help her daughter. She located a semi trained medic, who stitched up Erika's chin. The injury left a large, lifelong scar. In the past, Birzai had a hospital and a number of physicians, but there were none left. The physicians had either fled or had been conscripted by the Soviet or Nazi military to serve their armies as physicians.

While we were in Papilys, a German officer came to visit us and oversee our work on a regular basis. He brought a young dachshund puppy with him that yelped and chased not only the turkey chicks, but us kids. Looking back, I think the puppy, called Hexe (witch), was teething, and so she bit everyone and everything. She terrified me with those sharp, little teeth. At times, the officer left the puppy for several days. Sister Rita was scared to have her stay. She worried that if anything happened to this unruly pup; we would be blamed and would feel the consequences. But, over time, we saw less of this perpetually moving pup.

I don't remember going to school while we were in Lithuania. We went to church on Sundays in Papilys, the same old church my father had been baptized in, his father had ministered to, and even my sister Rita had been baptized in, while my father served as a deacon. This was an old church that had been built in 1578–1600. My parents had many old friends and acquaintances in this old town and on the surrounding farms. They were happy to see our family again and did not judge us to be Nazi collaborators. They understood why we had fled the Soviets.

They shared their experiences of life under the Soviets. There had been mass deportations to Siberia in June 1941. The men were either executed or sent to hard-labor camps. Women and children were transported to Siberia in boxcars. Their journeys went in stages, with stopovers in various places where they changed from trains to river barges and, later, either trucks or horses and sleighs.

We learned that my mother's brother, Jonas Rimkevicius; his wife, Jule; and their three children, daughter Aldona (fifteen), son Albinas (fourteen), and son Algis (six or seven), were among those deported to Siberia. Their father was arrested and sent to a labor camp. Then the rest of the family was sent to deep Siberia by the delta of the Lena River. Algis died from hunger and exposure during the first winter. Their journey had taken about three months.

The general population who remained in Lithuania during the Soviet occupation suffered in many ways. Property was confiscated, farms were collectivized, and the press and mail were censored. Midnight inspections by the NKVD (secret police) and searches of people's homes or apartments were common occurrences that one could not protest. Religious practices were greatly discouraged. Those who practiced religion by attending religious services could not hold any administrative or government jobs, such as teachers, mayors, postmasters, etc. People had to belong to the Communist party to be able to practice their professions. It was hard to know who was a true friend or who would denounce you the next day. Everybody was guarded.

The Lithuanian Evangelical Reformed Church in Papilys, Lithuania, 1927

Entrance to the church in Papilys, photo 2000

Close-up of architectural monument plaque of this
church built in 1578-1600. Photo,2000.

Fleeing

Our stay in Lithuania was short-lived, two months at the most. We enjoyed our return to Lithuania and a sense of freedom. We started hearing a persistent rumbling noise to the north. When we inquired about this, we were told that the German military was clearing out pockets of resistors and freedom fighters. But the rumbling, thunder noise persisted, and our father set off to Birzai to see if he could get clearer information.

Renate remembers when my father came to Birzai. It was her birthday, July 1, 1944, when she turned twelve. My father returned the same day after consulting with the Barnelis family and other friends in town. They all agreed that it was time to flee the Soviets again. The Nazi front was retreating, and the rumbling noise was Russian artillery. We packed our meager belongings and set off to Birzai, our county center. Our belongings and all seven family members were packed in a wagon drawn by two horses. In Birzai, we pulled into the yard where my paternal grandmother had lived. Soon the Barnelis family, with Aunt Fele aboard, pulled in with their covered wagon. As the day wore on, more and more wagons arrived. Somewhere between twenty and thirty wagons had gathered by nightfall.

As soon as we arrived in Birzai, my mother set off to Nemunelio-Radviliskis, to see her father and persuade him to come with us. Her father could not be persuaded to leave Lithuania and his home. He had survived the first occupation and thought that because of his age, he was safe. Mother returned tired and disappointed that her father refused to join us.

After spending the night sleeping in the barn, our convoy of twenty to thirty covered wagons set off toward Germany to escape the advancing Soviet Army. The fairly constant rumbling in the background increased our fear. The wagons were loaded to the hilt with essentials, family members, and all the food supplies we possessed. The convoy traveled down country roads during the day. In the evening, we stopped and unhitched and hobbled the horses and allowed them to graze in the meadow. Mothers started campfires and prepared meals from their available food supply. As we crossed Lithuania, we came across abandoned farms and large estates, whose inhabitants had fled for safety ahead of us. These were good resting places for the night. But the fear remained throughout the night: the horses could be stolen, bandits could rob us, or partisans could attack us because we were seen as "German collaborators." In the morning, the covered-wagon train started up again. Mothers preparing breakfast, men and older boys hitched up the horses, and the slow trek started again. If a wagon had to stop because of a breakdown, the whole train came to a standstill. It was slow going.

The road came to an end at Lithuania's biggest river, Nemunas, which became a big obstacle. Though both banks were steep, the river was fairly shallow, so we decided that our convoy would cross at this place. The horses and wagons struggled to get down the steep bank without overturning. Luckily, the river was shallow enough so that the horses did not have to swim, and we crossed the river without unloading the wagons and passengers. But the steep bank on the other side presented more problems. Some horses were unable to pull their loads up the bank. The horses were then unhitched from a wagon that had successfully crossed the river and conquered the uphill bank. These horses were harnessed as an additional team to help the wagon to make it up the bank. It took all day to cross, and both horses and men were exhausted. The next day we started moving again toward the southwest, to the German border.

It took more than three weeks to reach the border. We were stopped by the German military, and a sorting-out process was started once again. All the men and boys above a certain age were detained along with the horses and wagons. Women and children were put on trains and sent further inland in East Prussia. My sister Rita, at this time only fourteen years of age, was separated from our family, because the Nazi bureaucracy required her to attend a German high school. She was sent with our aunt Ona Ycas and cousin Onyte Ycas, who was seventeen, to Giessen, in western Germany. Two of Aunt Ona's sons were inducted in the German Army, and, as a reward, she was sent to inner Germany. I don't know how all these decisions were made and how the hundreds and thousands of fleeing people were sorted out or where they were sent.

The men and horses remained at the border under the supervision of the German defense forces. Their job was to dig trenches to hold back the Soviet tanks and artillery. There were hundreds and thousands laboring with shovels and other hand tools to build these defense fortifications that proved useless in the coming months. There were also women among these laborers, but I don't know how they were selected. Our father and Fritzas Barnelis were held back at this location.

So our mother, nanny Ane, Stasys, Jonas, and I continued the journey by train. We were lucky that the Barnelis family, mother Birute, her daughters Renate and Erika, as well as our Aunt Fele, were assigned to the same train car and destination. Being with at least some of our relatives gave us a small sense of security. We were not told what our destination would be. Again, we had no say about our lives. Our lives were at the mercy of the Third Reich policies and bureaucracy. Rita was also separated from us, and her whereabouts and fate were unknown at the time.

Drawing by cousin, Onyte of our covered wagon, when we are fleeing
Lithuania from the advancing Soviet front in 1944, dated July 17, 1944

Inside the covered wagon: cousin, Renate, and brother, Stasys are sitting, while aunt,
Fele is sleeping on the floor. Drawing by cousin, Onyte Ycas, dated July 22, 1944

East Prussia

THE RAILROAD STATION WHERE WE were dropped off was named Katzenellbogen. It was somewhere near Gotenhafen, presently Gdynia, East Prussia. A farmer with a wagon, drawn by two horses, met us at the station and took us with all the belongings we could carry to an empty small house that stood in a fenced yard. It was eerie entering this empty house that had no furniture and no belongings except a cooking stove that was directly opposite the only entrance door. There were no other doors, but there was a room to the right and one to the left of the kitchen area. There were a couple of small windows in these side rooms and several empty bed frames. The Barnelis family and Aunt Fele settled in the room to the right, the Neimanas family to the left. We hung up sheets in the room entrances for privacy.

The next day, this farmer brought us straw so that we could make straw mattresses. Apparently he was responsible for us to some extent. We wondered about the rightful owners of this small homestead. We knew that something tragic had happened to them. Were they Jewish? Were they political dissidents? Were they eliminated (killed)? Were they in labor camps? Were they in concentration camps? We felt like intruders on their tragedy. We spoke in whispers about the possible fate of the victims of this modest homestead.

The following day, we examined our current "home." Further in the yard, there was a freestanding brick oven that had been used for baking bread and other goods. It was heated by wood. There was a chicken coop, which we modified to become our outhouse. The outhouse was far away, especially in cold and rainy weather, but that just how it was. In the back of the dwelling were fruit trees, primarily cherry and plum. It was the end of summer and the beginning of harvest time, so most of the fruit was gone. This small orchard became our favorite refuge. We climbed the cherry trees and found congealed cherry sap, which we chewed like candy. The cherry trees were our gym as well; we climbed them and sat in their branches reading whatever we could find. Our nanny Ane managed to hang on to her hymn book. She sat by a cherry tree and sang our familiar church hymns softly to herself. At times, some of us children would join her. She was deeply devout, without ever judging others or expecting them to have her strong faith.

Our mother, nanny Ane, and Birute were expected to help the farmer with the harvest. In exchange, we went in the morning with a small pitcher to get milk from the farmer, and, occasionally, we even got a few eggs. The adults figured out how to use the outdoor oven and we baked our own bread. Nearby was a beech-tree grove, where we gathered the small beechnuts to enrich the baked goods. It was a big and tedious job to shell these small triangular seeds, but it gave us something to do in the evenings. There were large forests in this region, where I went with my mother to gather any blueberries and mushrooms we could find, but these were not plentiful. The soil was sandy and dry, and the mushrooms did not thrive.

In time, we made friends with the farmer's children, two girls and a younger boy. They came to our place and we played all kinds of games: hide-and-seek, volleyball without a net, catch, and whatever we could think of. But summer vacation came to an end, and Renate, Stasys, and

I had to go to school. It was several kilometers to the schoolhouse in Koeln. Soon Renate and Stasys were transferred to Kaunas German High School in Exile. This school was located on the Hela Peninsula in the Baltic Sea. It had been transferred from Kaunas in Lithuania during the evacuation from Lithuania. The girls lived and studied in one building and the boys in a separate building. However the mathematics courses were taught together in the boys' school. Here Renate and Stasys got to see one another and visit. Hela was a significant distance from Koeln; you had to get to a railroad station about five kilometers from Koeln, and then travel by train.

I remained in the small school in our village. I was miserable. I did not know any of the children. The teacher wore an SA (Sturm Abteilung) uniform and this, in itself, frightened me. We had to salute, "Heil Hitler," when he walked into the classroom. He sometimes made the whole class line up in a semicircle in front of the room. Standing in front of us, he asked questions from our assignments. Students who did not have the correct answer were slapped. I did not get slapped, but I was terrified and refused to continue going to school. Going to school was a requirement though, and our whole family could be punished. I don't know where my mother found a pack of cigarettes, but she went with me to the school and requested to speak to the teacher in private. She bribed him with the cigarettes so that I would not be slapped. Money did not have much value anymore; bribery and exchange of goods was better than currency.

It was a relatively quiet time for us. This little house was several kilometers from the village of Koelln, and, aside from going to school, my mother only went to town with ration cards to purchase basic goods. There was no military around during the fall, and only a few SA party members in the village. The constant fear of being overheard or reported to the authorities for unpatriotic words or behavior decreased, but our uncertainty about our fate and the whereabouts and living conditions of our family members increased greatly. There was no radio or newspapers, and whatever news we heard was through word of mouth and was not necessarily accurate. Mail was practically nonexistent, and every letter was censored.

So one day when our father showed up and brought with him two pairs of skis, we were overjoyed. His stay was only for a couple of days, but we were reassured that he was alive. He also brought us news that Rita was living with our aunt, Ona Ycas and her daughter, Onyte, in Giessen, West Germany, and was attending a German gymnasium (high school). We were overjoyed. Fritzas Barnelis also got a few days furlough after a near fatal attack while working on fortifications at the border. The "Volksturm" had already been established at this time. It consisted of all boys and from age sixteen to sixty-five, sworn in to defend the German Reich with whatever means were available. They had no uniforms and only a few had weapons. The rest were expected to fight the enemy with whatever was at hand: pitch forks, axes, fire, etc.

Although it was quiet around our little hut, at night we saw more frequent bombings of cities we judged to be around Danzig and Gotenhafen. We sometimes saw defense searchlights in the sky, lighting up airplanes and antiaircraft firings, and we heard distant explosions. The sky lit up in that area from burning factories, warehouses, and buildings. One night, we were watching a "star" that appeared to detach itself from the sky and move in our direction. Before long, as it got brighter and brighter, we realized it was a burning airplane that was descending fast. We heard a roar. We dropped to the floor; everything lit up; and, a few seconds later we heard a crash and an explosion. The airplane had hit the ground close by; the light from the burning plane was still visible. We wondered if there were any survivors but were too afraid to stumble in the dark across fields and unpaved roads. In the morning, we saw the charred and broken airplane in the field right behind our neighbor's house. The British Air force insignia was clearly visible. There were no survivors.

Soon there was snow on the ground, and the hilly landscape provided a great opportunity to try out the skis that my father had brought us. We did not have ski boots, and the bindings on the skis were not adjustable. Our attempts at skiing and staying on the skis involved more stumbles and falls than glides. We invited our neighbor's children to play with us and try out the skis. Their attempts were no more successful than ours. Finally we settled on keeping both skis together, sitting down on them and going downhill like on a toboggan. The days were sunny, and we played for hours. It was the most fun we had in a long time.

The winter settled in early in 1944, and the snow was well above our knees, roads were not plowed, and drifting snow had covered some roads completely. We could not tell where the banks or shoulders were, and if we stepped off the banks, we found ourselves up to our waists in snow. It was dangerous to go any distance from our home. It was in such weather that our neighboring farmer came to take us to another location. We wondered who ordered this move. Why were we moved? He loaded all of us into the sleigh with our meager belongings and took us to the nearest village, named Koellnerhutte. He took us to the village's schoolhouse, which was abandoned, and this became our next shelter.

The schoolhouse was a two-story building, so we had more space, but it was eerie living there. We wondered why it had been abandoned. Where were the children? What had happened to the teachers? There was a good-sized school yard to the back of the building. The playground ended at a rather steep hill, which was higher than the school. I do not remember going anywhere outside this yard while we stayed here. We wondered if our father knew we had been moved. Did brother Stasys and Renate, who were still in school on the Hela Peninsula, know that we had been moved? It was near Christmas and bitter cold. We felt completely cut off and with no means of communication or transportation. Luckily there was plenty of wood left in the supply building in the school yard. In the school itself, a good furnace in the basement heated both floors. The warm air rising from through the duct heated a wall covered with tile. We all gathered close to it to eat and stay warm.

We celebrated Christmas 1944 in this empty, desolate schoolhouse. It was a sad Christmas for us as our families were separated. We felt isolated, cold, and hungry. There was no Christmas tree, but we gathered by the warm wall, held hands, and sang "Silent Night" in Lithuanian.

Then one day, our father appeared. We were overjoyed that he was back with us, all in one piece, and our fear and worry subsided a bit. Now that our father was back with us, the next goal was to get our brother Stasys and cousin Renate back from school on the Hela Peninsula. Our father told us that the Soviet Army was continuing to gain ground, that the Nazi German Army was in retreat, and that there were refugees on trains and roads. He felt there was no time to lose, and he set off for the Hela Peninsula on the Baltic Sea to pick up Stasys and Renate He traveled on foot, and then by train, to reach the Hela Peninsula, where both were stranded.

Cousin Renate remembers that while they attended classes and living at Kauno German Gymnasium in Exile, they heard distant guns. They were glad to see our father and to leave their school. They boarded a train in Putzig, East Prussia, to go to Gotenhafen (Gdynia). Here they transferred to another train. Cousin Renate relates that they sat in the station a long time. It was cold, and they were very hungry. Our father pulled several pieces of bread and bacon out of his pocket. She still remembers how wonderful it tasted and how it satisfied their growling bellies. While waiting for their train, they saw passenger trains and freight trains crammed with refugees. Some traveled in open flat cars and were dead. Eventually their train arrived, bound for their destination, Katzenelbogen, East Prussia. From there they traveled on foot for another five kilometers. They were exhausted, cold, and hungry as they entered the schoolhouse. We hugged and cried in relief to be together again.

Cousin Renate related that one night she prayed very hard for her father to return to all of us. She fell asleep but awoke around midnight, hearing a knocking sound. Her prayer was answered, and her father had returned with a wagon and two horses. Next morning, Fritzas, Renate's father, urged us all to pack up and head for the Lautenburg train station as soon as possible. We were cut off from our nearest train station by military and refugee congestion trying to get to Gotenhafen. The country roads were covered by deep snow, and one wagon, even with a team of horses, could not pull both our families with our measly belongings. So both my father and cousin Renate's father went to find a farmer who had a sleigh and was willing to take us to Lautenburg (currently Leborg, Poland). Fritzas gave the farmer Renate's winter coat and a bicycle as payment.

We set out around the middle of January 1945, bundled up with whatever we possessed, covered with blankets in an open wagon and an open sleigh. The beginning was slow, the horses straining to pull the wagon through deep snow and drifts. The sleigh with runners had an easier time moving in snow and ice, so it led the way.

After many hours, we got to a larger paved road that, although snow-covered, had been cleared, and the driving became easier. As the road went around a downhill curve with some shrubs and trees on the right side, we spotted some dark green material partially covered by snow under a small evergreen tree. We stopped both wagon and sleigh. I remember running across the road to have a look, my mother beside me.

As we cleared the snow off, we realized that it was a person. I believe it was a woman. She had been shot, and there was a bullet hole and some blood visible. I have no recollection of what was said or how long we stood there, but we left her covered by snow where she lay.

We continued down the road, and I felt numb, with thoughts and questions racing through my head. I just wanted to get away from there, to get to the train. Several kilometers down the road, a tin mess kit lay in the middle of the road, and then, just a little further on, a body dressed in black-and-white striped clothing lay by the road. The person was dead. Some family members, including Renate, got out of the wagonand walked beside it. I did not.

We continued on. There were more dropped mess kits and more bodies pulled off the road. We didn't stop anymore. We just continued, ever so slowly. Then soon there were more bodies, but they had not even been pulled off the road. "Stutthof," the name of a large concentration camp in East Prussia (now Poland), was printed on their uniforms. They were on a forced march and died from exhaustion, starvation, disease, and exposure, and were shot when they could no longer walk. They died from cruelty.

We continued and came to a small town toward evening, but it was not yet dark. There were no people or children on the streets. It was deadly quiet. As we approached a church, we saw some armed German soldiers. Then we saw the churchyard fence. Inside the fence stood Stutthof concentration-camp inmates in just their striped uniforms in freezing weather. There was complete silence. Exhausted, starved human beings stared at us. We looked and lowered our eyes, feeling horrified, helpless, and outraged, but we continued our journey.

It was already dark when we stopped for the night at the outskirts of town. We were cold, hungry, and tired. I don't know if it was just luck or if the farmer with the sleigh knew the two brothers who offered us shelter. It felt wonderful to be in a warm place. The farmer stayed to warm up and set off for home. The two brothers made us feel welcome and treated us like guests. They prepared warm food and entertained us with stories about themselves. They were truly hospitable. One brother had been a wine waiter in a large hotel in Koeln (currently Cologne, Germany); the other had lived in Lautenburg and was a shoemaker. They were such a contrast to our shocking experience of witnessing total disregard and cruelty to human beings. Kindness and compassion still existed.

The next morning, the brothers took us all in the wagon to the train station. For their hospitality and their help, our parents gave them the wagon with the team of horses.

The Train Ride

THE BROTHERS DROPPED US OFF at the freight-train station. Passenger trains were no longer running in this region. There were only unscheduled freight trains, and military trains had priority. Our father and Renate's father approached some armed soldiers who were guarding one of the trains. I don't know how they bargained and how the conversation went, but the soldiers agreed to let our families board a boxcar. The price for it was a bicycle, several gold coins my father had sewn into his coat, his fur coat, and some real coffee beans that my mother had stashed away. The soldiers unlocked the boxcar door and we clambered in with our worldly bundles. Then the soldiers locked the door again. It was dark and cold, but we were on a train that promised to take us into Germany, away from the Communists. It turned out that this was an ammunition train bound for the West Front. There were actual bombs in our boxcar.

The train stood in the station for quite some time, and we settled ourselves close to the door, one family on one side of the door, and the other family on the other. The train eventually started moving. When the train stopped, the soldiers opened the heavy sliding boxcar door and we could see where we were. Often the train stopped in some fields and, at other times, in a train station along a passenger platform. In the train stations, there were always several women with the Red Cross sign, tending huge kettles of soup. The Red Cross workers doled out ladles of soup to the thousands of refugees fleeing the East Front and to the wounded soldiers being transported to the West. These platforms were crowded with people, children, and soldiers. More refugees boarded, and our boxcar filled with people. Everyone was trying to get away from the approaching Soviet front, and many did not have a definite destination. We were hoping to get to Giessen, Germany, where we hoped to be reunited with our sister Rita and Aunt Ona and her daughter, Onyte.

The train stopped more frequently in some open fields rather than at train stations and we never knew how long we would be standing. Sometimes it was for hours, others briefly to let another train pass us. Bombings of cities and railroads were a daily occurrence, leading to unpredictable stops and meaningless train schedules.

Our families huddled close together, sitting on our bundles and bombs. (Maybe they were disarmed?) None of us remember exactly how many days it took us to get to Stettin (currently Szczecin, Poland), a big industrial city. When the train guards opened the door to our car, we saw that we had pulled into a huge railroad yard, with dozens of tracks and standing trains. This was a freight-train yard, and we clambered or jumped down, glad to stretch our legs and move around.

It was still light, and my brother, Stasys; cousin Renate; and I went around various trains looking for anything edible or useful. We found a car loaded with cabbage and picked up several heads, but, sadly, they were frozen and inedible. Then we saw a tank train with soldiers and people milling around it. It looked like the people were standing in line. Someone had found a valve and discovered that this tank car was filled with alcohol. We quickly ran back to our car and got any container that could hold liquid. We got in line and were lucky to get some of the alcohol and bring it back. Although we were just children, we got several sips. We tried to go back, but we found an armed guard had been posted, and the tap was turned off.

Sirens went off as night fell, and search lights crisscrossed the sky. Soldiers came to our boxcar and told us to go to the air shelter. There were no lights, and we didn't know exactly where the air shelter was, but we stumbled on, following the crowd ahead of us. Finally we reached the underground bunker that was already filled with people. We crowded in, with people behind us pushing and also seeking shelter. The door was closed, and it was pitch dark inside.

We could still hear the sirens, and then the antiaircraft shells and bombs exploding. We sat in fear, hoping the bombs would not hit the ammunition train we were traveling on. It was scary in the bunker. Some children were crying, some people prayed. There was no place to sit; we were wedged in between total strangers. The air smelled of human sweat, vomit, and human waste. Renate stepped into some waste, but there was no way to clean up. Time stood still. All ears were listening for the all clear. When it finally came, the door was opened, and some light came in. Now people pushed to get out, get some air, and see what the damage was.

It was cold and dark, but not like in the bunker, and we found our train undamaged. The bombing had taken place more in the industrial part of Stettin, and we escaped unscathed once again. Finally our train got rolling, and our mood lightened. It would have been nice if there had been windows so that we could have at least seen the landscape and the towns we passed, but this was a closed boxcar. Brother Stasys peeked through a crack in the door and saw the train-station name, Halle.

Pretty soon the train came to a stop, and we were in Pasewalk, Germany. Here we were told to get out of the military train and board a passenger train. The station and the platforms were filled with a multitude of people: young, old, wounded soldiers, children, armed soldiers, and Red Cross workers with steaming kettles of some kind of soup. At least we got something warm in our stomachs.

I have no idea how we got tickets or how we knew what platform to go to. Our families wanted to get to Weimar, Germany, where Birute Barnelis's sister, Danute Kregzde, and her husband, Jokubas, lived. We waited on a platform until the train arrived. The train was already crowded, and the mass of people waiting on the platform surged forward, pushing and shoving one another. We were part of that crowd, and I hung on to my mother's coat as hard as I could. I was not quite ten years old at this time, and I was terrified to be left behind by myself.

Nanny Ane carried Johnny so he wouldn't get trampled. Luckily our family and the Barnelis family got on the same car. There was no sitting room, and the aisles between the seats as well as the passageways were filled with suitcases, bundles, and people sitting on them or standing between belongings. Eventually we arrived in Weimar, and our families, as well as many other passengers, got off the train.

We remained on the platform with our suitcases and bundles. It was obvious that the station had been bombed recently; bombed cars and locomotives in shambles littered the train station. Only a few tracks were intact and operating. Fritzas Barnelis and Renate set off to find our cousin and her husband, Jokubas. Fritzas' wife, Birute Barnelis; daughter, Erika; Aunt Fele; and their belongings remained with our family on the platform. Both Erika and Johnny sat on top of our belongings, while we anxiously waited for the return of Fritzas and Renate.

In the meantime, people milled around and passed on anything newsworthy. A large presence of armed soldiers patrolled up and down the train tracks and platforms. The large concentration camp Buchenwald was in the outskirts of Weimar, and people on the platform told us that some prisoners had escaped. They said soldiers were on a lookout for them because they were dangerous, and we should be careful. We listened but did not say anything and were probably more afraid of the armed soldiers than any escaped concentration-camp prisoners.

Eventually Fritzas and Renate returned. They had found Danute and Jokubas, but both advised us to continue our journey. They had come to Weimar, Germany, sometime in 1943. The exact circumstances of how they left Kaunas, Lithuania, are not known. Jokubas was a veterinarian; Danute was a dentist. While they were in Weimar, Jokubas worked as a meat inspector. They had been able to stay in touch by mail with Aunt Ona Ycas in Giessen. They told Fritzas and Renate that Giessen had been severely bombed. Because of the bombing and the continued danger of bombing, the high school (gymnasium) had been relocated to a village called Holzheim. This is where Aunt Ona; her daughter, Onyte; and our sister Rita were living. Jokubas and Danute urged us to proceed by train to Licht, and then find our way to Holzheim.

The platform where we waited became more and more crowded. As the train approached, people pushed and shoved to get in position to get on the train. By the time the train stopped, we could see that it was already carrying passengers. The pushing and shoving increased. I held on to nanny Ane's hand, my mother carried Johnny, and our father and Stasys carried most of our bundles. The Barnelis family was also struggling to get on the train. They were assisting Aunt Fele, who was elderly and rather helpless. Somehow we all made it on the train, but not into the same car. This was a passenger train, and every nook was filled. These passengers were not vacationers. They were women; children; a few older men; and an occasional wounded soldier, probably on leave, all trying to get away from the Eastern Front. Those who got a seat were lucky; the rest of us stood or sat on our parcels. There was some grumbling, but most were exhausted and glad to be on the train.

I cannot say how long this last leg of our train ride lasted or how we knew where to get off, but we all got off at Licht, Germany. Again, our father and Fritzas Barnelis bartered for transportation while we waited in the train station. It felt good to be able to move and to be out of the rumbling, crowded train. Our fathers were successful in getting a farmer to take us to Holzheim with his horses and wagon. We all climbed in, still wearing our winter clothes.

I was hot and sticky, not having washed during the whole trip. We were a good distance south and west from our last "home," and it felt like the beginning of spring. It felt good to breathe fresh air and be out of the constant sound of train wheels and the crush of the crowd.

Finally we entered a village. We saw a church steeple and the street surfaced with cobblestones. There were homes with wide gates on both sides of the road, so a horse team could enter with a fully loaded wagon. We proceeded until we came to an open square with a water pump, a manure pit, and many white geese wandering around. There were at least three other streets that ran into this square. One street to our right went slightly uphill, and we turned into it. Rita was running down the cobbled street with her pigtails flying and her arms outstretched.

Holzheim

—

OUR FAMILY WAS OVERJOYED TO be together again after many months
of separation. Our brother, Johnny, remembered Rita running down the
narrow street with outstretched arms. There was hugging, kissing, and
crying with relief to be together again, even if the future was completely
unknown. We were rejoicing in the moment, feeling the family closeness;
nothing else mattered at that moment.

Through the local administration, we were assigned living space. The
local bureaucracy was still functioning despite the severe impact of the war.
The Neimanas were assigned to the Jung household, where Rita had been
placed by the school. We were a large family of seven, so our mother, father,
and our brother Stasys were allocated sleeping space in the Frau Zeiss home
across the street. Frau Zeiss was an elderly widow who was rather resentful
and suspicious of our intrusion, but all had to make adjustments because of
the war. There were many refugees fleeing from the Eastern Front.

Frau Jung seemed quite a bit friendlier. There were no men in her
household either, but she had several children and managed the household
and farm. We had a room on the main floor with a wood burning heater.
This is where our family gathered for meals and spent time together. This
room had a window to the street through which we could see Frau Zeiss's
home and the activity on the street. Rita, nanny Ane, Johnny, and I slept

at the Jungs' house. Our first night was like a dream; we slept in real beds, and not just beds, but down beds. It was like sinking into a cloud and being covered by warm wings. I slept with Rita, and it was wonderful to cuddle up and be close.

The Barnelis family was assigned to the Jaeger family household. This was a relatively well-to-do farmer who even had horses. This household was further up the road through which we had entered Holzheim but within easy walking distance from the Jung household. I believe that our aunt Fele initially lived with them, but later she had her own room in a different household.

In the morning, when we got up, we wanted to bathe after weeks of wearing the same clothes in all kinds of conditions. It came as a great surprise and disappointment that people in Holzheim did not have bath-tubs or showers. They only took sponge baths. They were bathed when they were born and when they were married. This seemed rather odd to us, but we had to make the best of the situation and adapt. We moved a large metal tub into our living room, filled it with heated water, and bathed ourselves as best as we could. The way of life in Holzheim had many surprises for us.

The farmers' homesteads were built in a rectangular fashion, with a wide, double gate in the middle for farming purposes and a small door for people to enter at the side. As you entered the homestead, the living quarters, either one or two stories high, were usually to one side. On the other side of the gate were the barn holding hay, straw, animal feed, and farming equipment. At a right angle, there was another structure for vari-ous uses, and the stable for livestock ran parallel to the street. Next to the stable was a pit for manure, which the farmers used to fertilize their fields in spring and fall, which drew thousands of flies in the summer. This was a big surprise to us, for we had never seen manure kept so close to living quarters. Households on a street adjoined one another, so there was no space between the structures, nor was there empty space behind, as other homesteads butted into them.

Most households were run by women, as there were few men around—probably because of the war. All adult women wore floor-length black dresses with multiple underskirts. They also had braids arranged in various fashions or buns on the back of their head. Girls wore regular clothes, mostly knee-high socks and knee-length dresses, but they also wore braids. Women drove oxen or cow teams, worked the stables, milked the cows, and raised chickens for eggs and geese to fatten for Christmas. They spun their own wool and knitted all kinds of clothing. They also tended their vegetable gardens and farm fields. School children helped on their free days. During summer vacations and at harvest time, everyone pitched in.

There were a few stores in the village. We could get meat with food stamps at the butcher shop. The lines were very long, and it was not unusual to stand in line for several hours and then only get a fraction of the allowed portion. There was a general store, where we bought washing powder and matches and a few other items that were available. A bakery was located toward the end of the village, where we could buy bread with bread coupons. The line there was not quite so long, and the smell coming from it was mouth-watering. What we liked best about this bakery was that it provided free service to the village population on Saturdays. Village residents prepared their yeast bread and coffee-cake dough the night before. Early on Saturday mornings, women and girls carried pans of formed bread and coffee cakes dressed with fruit to the bakery. They carried the pans on top of their heads, and we watched in amazement as none stumbled or lost their pans. Then the wonderful smell of fresh-baked bread spread through the streets, and, in the afternoon, the villagers carried their freshly baked goods home to be enjoyed the following day.

Sundays started out early, and all residents put on their best clothing. Soon the church bells rang, and people started leaving their homes. Then we heard a church bell from another village, and then another. It became a wonderful chorus, a special hymn that seemed to unify the world and speak of peace. Everyone went to church, and all villagers in this area were Lutherans, so we felt quite comfortable with the church services. After the Sunday lunch, there was a regular coffee hour when women would take turns hosting a *Klatsch* (gossip) hour to catch up with the town news and enjoy the freshly baked coffee cakes.

No radios or newspapers were available in Holzheim. So on weekdays, toward evening, a town crier walked to designated areas and rang a hand bell. People came out on the street or opened their windows while he read the official news about the war progress. We all came out to listen and to chat with our neighbors. Children then spent some time playing on the street, skipping rope, playing hopscotch, rolling bicycle wheels down the hill with a stick, and playing with homemade spinning tops. Somehow I felt more included and enjoyed the games. War seemed far away.

There were many shortages because of the war: clothing, shoes, shelter, medicines, and even salt, but the most intensely felt shortage was food. We were lucky that it was spring, and we could plant a vegetable garden on the small plot assigned to us by village officials. But it takes time to grow vegetables, and we had to depend on the goodwill and generosity of the villagers. At times our father bartered for food with some of our few possessions or labored in exchange for food. We tended our small garden plot with great care. We acquired a little handcart, loaded it up with water in various containers and some improvised hand tools for weeding, hoeing, and digging. We looked for insects and picked them off by hand. Spring lettuce was the first reward and gift for our efforts.

It was a beautiful spring green and tasted wonderfully fresh with a little bit of sour cream. Over time, we got more rewards for our efforts: onions, radishes, spinach, turnips, carrots, beets, and wonderful tomatoes, as well as cabbage and Brussels sprouts, which I had never seen before.

As spring progressed, we noticed more German troop activity. Trucks and troops moved through the village, most activity taking place at night. Then we started hearing bombers droning at night. At times we heard bombs exploding at some distance. At the same time, strafe airplanes began flying over the village, across fields, and along highways, attacking with machine guns anything or anyone who moved. We couldn't hear the strafe airplanes coming, so we couldn't take shelter as we could when we heard the bombers droning. These planes were fast and appeared without warning right on top of us. People tried to stay out of sight as much as they could, but life continued, and essential tasks had to be done.

One day, when nanny Ane, brother Stasys, and cousin Renate had gone to the nearby forest to gather firewood for cooking and heating, they were overtaken by a strafing attack. As they were going along a road pulling the little handcart, they heard bullets flying. They dropped into the ditch along the road as the plane flew over them, spitting bullets. Luckily, no one was hurt, but all were badly shaken up. It was a close call.

One day during this period of strafe bombings, Stasys and I set off into the surrounding area of the village, looking for anything that might be edible or useful in some way. We mostly stayed off the roads and went along wooded areas to be less visible. As we went up a slow incline, we saw a vehicle standing in the field. We could not see anyone moving around it or in it. We dropped to the ground and watched the vehicle for, trying to make sure there were no soldiers there. We were sure that this was a military vehicle, because there were no private vehicles in the village. After a while, we started crawling toward it. The vehicle appeared to be burned. We wondered if there might be some explosive devices there, but we had to check it out as there might be something of value. As we crawled closer, we saw some brown, granular substance on the ground. What could this be?

We circled around the vehicle, also afraid there might be some injured or dead soldier inside, but no one was present. We finally stood up and examined our find closer. It was a burned-out field kitchen. We wondered what had happened to it. We knew it wasn't bombed, because it was fairly intact aside from being burned. We didn't find anything that could be salvaged aside from that dark-brown granular substance. We couldn't tell what it was. We figured that it was not explosive because it would have been gone. It could be poison, but this was a field kitchen and not likely to carry poison, so we decided to taste it, although it looked icky. We both licked a finger and touched the substance, and then slowly touched it with our tongues. It was *salt*! We had not had salt for weeks, maybe months, and we couldn't buy it in stores. We did not have any containers, so how could we take it back home? We decided to go home for a container. We rushed home as fast as we could, elated about our find.

Our parents and nanny Ane were surprised and happy. It was a treasure. We could use it; we could share it with the Barnelis family; we could barter with it. But first, we had to bring it home. It had to be done in an unobtrusive way. Our parents decided that we should use backpacks, because pots or pails would be too obvious, and the villagers would want at least part of it. So Stasys and I set off with two backpacks and tools for shoveling. It was late afternoon, and we did not attract any attention as we set off again. We found the burned-out field kitchen, got down on our hands and knees, and shoveled the dirty brown salt into the backpacks. By the time our backpacks were full, they were heavy, and the sun was setting. We started back home, feeling like we had hit a gold mine and helped our family. There were no incidents on the way home; all was well.

The whole family gathered around us as we put the heavy sacks on the table. Our dad opened the backpacks with Mom and nanny Ane standing close by. Everyone was pleased and happy, and it was almost like a Christmas celebration. Now we had to figure out how to purify it. Dad took charge of that, as he had lived through many hardships and knew how to improvise things. He asked our mom and nanny Ane to round up the largest pots they could find. We picked out the large pieces of debris by hand, and dissolved the salty mess in water. As the salt dissolved, smaller debris pieces floated to the top. We skimmed off as much of the dirt as possible, and then strained the salt to remove the sediment. We put the large pot on the stove to evaporate the water. This process was repeated several times over a couple of days, until the salt was fairly clean and dry. It is amazing how much difference it made in the taste of anything and everything. The Barnelis family also enjoyed the marvelous taste of this lucky find.

The strafe bombers continued flying and attacking through Holzheim and the surrounding areas. At times we heard heavier bombings in towns some distance away. We considered ourselves lucky to have avoided heavy bombings so far. Then somehow, none of us can remember exactly how, we got word that the Americans were coming. We felt hopeful and glad that the war would come to an end. We thought of the Americans as liberators, but we were also fearful at how the transition would take place. There were still some German soldiers around. Would they surrender, or would they resist? Was there still some residual German military unit hiding nearby, and would a fight break out? We spent an anxious night, awake much of the time. Danger was still present.

Toward morning, motorized vehicles moved through the village. As we looked cautiously through the window, we saw jeeps, trucks, and American soldiers in the street. White sheets hung from every window that we could see—a sign of surrender! A voice on a loudspeaker told all residents to stay indoors and any German soldiers to come out onto the street and surrender. A few soldiers appeared on the street with their arms on their heads. They assembled in small groups in the square, were patted down for weapons, and were led away out of our sight. But we continued to hear movement of vehicles and voices, but not clearly enough to understand. The war was over!

Our whole family sat in our room, listening and not speaking. I remember sitting on my dad's lap, the safest place. For a while, all was still. Then we heard a crackling noise that sounded like mice running through straw. The crackling increased, and we had to look at what was happening. Who was the first to open the door into the courtyard to see what was causing the crackling? Our family went into the courtyard.. Fire shot out of the thatched roof that was attached to our building, and small tongues of flame were already licking our roof. Our landlord, the Jungs, opened the large double doors, and we ran out into the street.

My mother took Johnny and me across the narrow street, put Johnny's hand in mine, and told me to stay there. Then she ran back into the house with the rest of the household and started to carry out our belongings. I was holding on to Johnny, but I had a terrible fear of fire and started yelling at the top of my lungs. I was horrified. Then Johnny started to cry as well. My mother ran up to me, shook me firmly and said, "This is not the time to cry." She went back to saving what could be carried out of the house. The animals had to be moved as well. Neighbors gathered to help, and the American soldiers helped to put out the fire, which was more intense in the adjoining house. The American soldiers even helped to carry out the furniture.

Eventually the fire was put out, and the process was reversed, carrying everything back into the Jung's' homestead. We were fortunate as the fire had not severely damaged the Jung's home, and we did not lose any of our belongings. Through neighbors and village residents, we found out that some German soldiers had been hiding in the barn adjoining the Jung's home. They did not want to surrender, and the American soldiers had fired into the barn, setting it on fire. At this point, the Germans had surrendered. Nobody was killed in this action, but I believe a few were wounded.

The following day, announcements were made that all residents had to bring all weapons and cameras out of their homes and put them on the ground. The residents were to stand behind their weapons and cameras. Again we all piled out onto the street; we had neither weapons nor cameras. We could see a few old weapons but no cameras. The American soldiers picked up a few items, and then we were ordered to go inside.

For a few days, nothing moved in the street, except military jeeps and trucks. I don't know if we stayed inside because we were afraid to go out, or if we were ordered to remain indoors. Our family spent most of the time in the larger first-floor room. We peered out from behind lace curtains to see if anything was going on this narrow uphill street. A jeep with several soldiers inside bounced uphill on our cobblestone street. As it went past our window, we saw something shiny bounce out of the jeep and onto the street. We expected the jeep to stop and a soldier to retrieve the object, but it just kept on going. We wondered what the object might be. Could it be an explosive device? Could it be something important that the soldiers would come looking for? Was it something useful, maybe edible?

We waited a long while, and then nanny Ane said, "I will get it. What can they do to an old woman?" She quickly ran outside along the wall and was back in no more than a couple minutes. The object was a rectangular metal container about six inches high and four inches wide. It was beige on the sides, with English writing on it. The top and the bottom were shiny metal, which had reflected the sun as it bounced out of the jeep. We all wanted to look at it and hold it. None of us could read English, but we could tell by the feel of it that it contained a liquid. Could it possibly be gasoline for the jeep? We decided the container was too small for that. We still wondered if it could be an explosive substance, but decided that since it hadn't exploded when it hit the cobblestone, it was probably safe to handle. But how could we open it?

Our father decided to use a sharp object such as a large nail and a hammer to make a small opening. It worked, and an oily substance dripped out of it. I don't remember who tasted it, but it was some kind of cooking oil. We were delighted. It was an unexpected gift. Next morning, nanny Ane made pancakes for us. It was a celebration, since we had not had anything as tasty as pancakes for a long time.

Pretty soon life resumed much of its usual routine. The farmers went to the fields again, and we tended our little vegetable garden. The American military had established its headquarters and its mess hall in the building at the end of our street that had previously housed the relocated German gymnasium. The military was quite unobtrusive, and we did not feel threatened.

The greatest hardship for us at this time was hunger. We became foragers and scavengers. We scoured the forest and fields and meadows for edible wild foods to supplement our vegetables. In the forest, which was common property, we found a large growth of raspberries. We wore long-sleeved clothing so we could walk between the plants without getting too many scratches from the thorns. We returned for many weeks to get the ripened berries. We gathered mushrooms and a wild plant that was similar to spinach, but sour. After the cherry-tree owners harvested their bountiful yield, we got permission to pick the leftover fruit.

One day while we were hunting for mushrooms in the forest, we came upon the American military mess dump. This was a great find. We found a big piece of round cheese with about a third gone. It had some maggots in it, but we brought it home. We cut out the infested parts and still had enough cheese for delicious sandwiches with fresh vegetables. Some time during the summer, the farmers butchered their hogs. They were willing to share with us what they called, "Wurst Suppe". This was a broth made from pigs' intestines. It tasted awful, even though we suffered from hunger. We also started raising our own rabbits. These were not wild rabbits, but domesticated ones called "Kaninchen", which were raised for food. We could always gather enough wild weeds and bits of hay to feed them.

In the fall, after the fields were harvested for grains, the farmers permitted us to go over the fields and gather the leftover ears of grain. This was an undertaking for the whole family. We took pillowcases or any other fabric that could be used as a sack and walked down the rows of harvested wheat fields, picking up ears of wheat. It was an undertaking that we repeated each day for several weeks. We managed to gather quite a few sacks. The village miller ground our grain for us, and from then on we joined the Saturday parade to the bakery in the morning and back home in the afternoon with fresh-smelling bread and yeast cake. The great hunger was abated.

One day as Stasys was walking to Lang Goenz, the nearest railroad station, he found a hare in the middle of the road that had been run over by a car. He quickly picked up the rabbit and hid it in a field of turnips. On his way home from school, he picked up the rabbit and brought it home in his school pack. What a delicious surprise. Our mother did whatever needed to be done to get it ready for cooking. I was always squeamish about such things and did not want to see or hear about the skinning and preparation of meat. It turned out to be a great feast for us as we had meat, our own homegrown vegetables, and our own baked bread. Things were looking up.

After the harvest time, school started for us. Since Rita was going to a gymnasium or high school, she had to take a daily train to Giessen. Renate and Stasys also attended school in Giessen. They all had to walk about five kilometers to Lang Goenz, and then take the train to Giessen to get to their schools. I was the only one attending the school in Holzheim, as both Erika and Johnny were too young to attend school. This was a multigrade classroom. The instructor was a young man with a severe limp. I thought he had been a soldier who had been wounded in the German military and found unfit for continued service.

There were about thirty to forty boys and girls in the school classroom, sitting at their desks. We still used slate tablets and chalk for writing, math, and homework. Each morning, our teacher walked down the aisles between the school desks and looked at our work. If our work was found unsatisfactory, he would twist an ear, pull hair, or administer a slap. At times, he called a student to the front of the classroom to have one or both hands hit with a rod, or the student had to bend over and be whacked on the buttocks with the rod.

There was a boy, whose name I cannot remember, who was the most frequent recipient of punishment. For some reason, I judged him unable to learn and deficient in some way. I felt it was wrong and cruel when this boy was punished, because I believed we should protect and be kind to someone who was weaker or less capable. One day, he was again called up to the front of the room. He was told to bend over the teacher's desk, and the teacher paddled his buttocks with the rod. The classroom was silent. Suddenly I stood up, walked up the aisle between the desks, up to the teacher, and grabbed the rod. I threw it on the floor and walked out of the classroom, down the stairs, and out of the school building. Then I ran across the square and up the inclined street to home.

I knew I had caused problems for my parents again and felt bad about that. I told my mother what I had done, and then curled up in my bed. I cannot remember what my parents said, nor if there were any particular consequences for me in the school. Maybe my mother bribed the teacher or bought him off. Maybe there was leniency because the war had ended and the Nazis had lost the war. I continued going to that same classroom until we left Holzheim.

At this time, our family spent most of the daytime at Frau Zeiss's establishment, because there was more space in her yard, and this was also where we kept the cage for our rabbits. The elongated room attached to her home was cold and damp so that during the night, visible mold would grow on our shoes and on the walls. We had a small wood burning stove in that room, but it barely took the chill out of the air.

When apple trees and other fruit trees ripened, the village administration allocated trees that belonged to the Holzheim village to various families who did not have fruit trees. We were allocated an apple tree. Renate tells me that her family had plums and small pears. I don't know who the other families were, but we were glad we had apples. We picked all the apples we could and brought them home in sacks in the little handcart and on our backs. We brought them to Frau Zeiss's yard to make apple butter.

This was a community project. More women came from different households, and more children appeared. The apples were washed in big tubs and sorted. Chairs and benches were brought out so that the workers could sit while cutting up the apples. Several large kettles were set up for apples, ready for cooking. I can't remember how the fire was kept going under the kettles, but these kettles were going for hours and hours. There was no sugar, so the apples had to be cooked at a low heat for a long time, until they were brown, thick, caramelized, and sweet tasting. The mash had to be stirred all the time, and women took turns. This process lasted late into the night. In the morning, the apple butter was ladled into earthenware or enamel containers and divided up among the participants. Renate tells me they cooked plums with pears in their household. We knew we could store these fruit jams throughout the winter and have something delicious to put on our bread.

This happened close to my eleventh birthday, and my mother wanted to do something special for me, because I had outgrown most of my clothes. She took the Nazi German flag, which every resident in Germany had to possess along with Hitler's photograph or face reprimand and punishment during Hitler's rule. The Hitler photo had already been gone for quite some time, but the flag was made of good material, and my mother decided to make a dress out of it for my eleventh birthday. So when I got up, I found the bright red dress, embroidered in the front, and a sheet of paper with a poem written for me by my godfather, Fritzas Barnelis. I was overjoyed. I was so happy; I was hopping up and down. But at the moment, there was no one with whom to share my joy; all had gone to harvest potatoes. I got dressed in my bright red dress, picked up the poem, got our newly acquired bicycle, and set off for the potato field.

It was a bright day, with an intense blue sky. I pedaled through the village and along a farm road to where the rest of the family was. There was a little breeze and I felt like I was flying, brighter than a flag, with words of praise and love in my pocket. There could not be a better day.

Somewhat around this time Danute and Jokubas Kregzde arrived in Holzheim from Weimar after the Third Reich's unconditional surrender. They were assigned a small two-room apartment. Soon after that, Dr. Vaitaitis and his wife, Paulina, who was a dentist, and a close friend of Danute Kregzde, arrived in Holzheim as well. They were followed by the Sernas couple, Adomas and Edita, who were friends of our family in Lithuania. There was also the Kirkilionis family who lived in Holzheim. This family consisted of a father and three grown sons. I do not know how or why they came to this village, but, since they were Lithuanians, we all became friends. Mr. Kirkilionis was an expert basket weaver, and he taught my brother, Stasys, to weave baskets. Stasys spent quite a bit of time at their "apartment." I think he enjoyed the comradeship with other young men. But our favorite gathering place was at the Kregzdes' apartment. It was probably the smallest place, but this is where we crowded to play endless games of gin rummy, and chat.

As winter set in, we found out how cold the unheated bedrooms were, even if we had down beds. The room temperature was below freezing, and we would heat up a brick on the heating stove, wrap it in a towel or some other heavy material, and take it to bed with us. The brick helped warm our feet so we could fall asleep. In the morning when we woke up and wanted to wash up, we found the big washbowl and water pitcher that was present in every sleeping room covered with a thin sheet of ice. It was cold even to stick our fingers in the water and break the ice. One day, Rita took a heated brick wrapped in a towel and went to bed. She must have been in a deep sleep, because somehow she shifted the brick so that it touched her shin bone and caused a deep burn. This burn did not heal for months and was painful. She kept this scar for life.

We celebrated Christmas 1945 and New Year 1946 in Holzheim. We attended church, heard the church bells ring in the New Year, and were content that our lives were not in danger from day to day, although our future had no direction or permanence. Then somehow, our parents found out about the UNRA, United Nations Refugee Association, later known as DP camps (displaced persons camps). Our father made contact with them. The closest camp was located in Hanau. Neither brother Stasys, cousin Renate, or I know exactly what the application process involved, but we were registered as refugees. The camps were overcrowded with refugees from all of Europe, both east and west. Since we had living space and shelter, we were not admitted to the DP camp, but we were placed on the waiting list. There were war refugees from the slave-labor camps and concentration camps, and those trying to get out of the way of the battle zones who had neither shelter nor food. They were in far worse shape than our family and had priority for admission to the DP camps. But due to severe food shortages in Germany, we were eligible for CARE packages.

Our father traveled to Hanau at certain intervals and brought back a CARE package. It was a special occasion each time, and we gathered around the table to see what wonderful surprises the package held. There was powdered cacao, powdered milk, Spam, sardines, real coffee, sugar, canned potatoes, canned white corn, and a chocolate bar, the best item of all. There may have been other items, but I do not remember them. We felt grateful to receive these packages. Our life became easier, and we no longer visited the military mess dump.

Holzheim had offered us shelter during some of the bleakest times of the war, but there was no future there for us. We did not belong there. Now that the war had ended, we wanted to be back in the Lithuanian community. We had never considered ourselves German, and our experience of the last five years left us more convinced than ever that we were Lithuanians.

Toward the end of summer of 1946, we received word from the DP camp administration, that we were eligible for admission. I don't know exactly what the admission process entailed, but both of our parents had to present documents to the admitting committee proving that we were indeed refugees from Lithuania. We were happy and relieved that we would be living with our people. But leaving Holzheim was bittersweet as we were leaving our relatives, the Barnelis family, Danute and Jokubas, and other friends behind, and we weren't sure if or when we would ever see one another again. Holzheim had provided us with shelter during some of the most severe bombing and fighting of WWII. The displaced persons camp did not guarantee a rosy future, but it offered hope.

Drawing by sister, Rita, 1944, of Turngasse, on which we lived, the Jung's household on the right and Zeiss's home on left. The relocated High School from Giessen is at the end of the street

Turngasse in Holzheim: Jung's household is on the
right side and Zeiss's on left. Photo,2000.

Main street in Holzheim in 2000. Little has changed except
for pavement of streets, which are black topped.

Lutheran church on Main street in Holzheim, 2000.

Hanau

Our family arrived in Hanau, West Germany, in late summer 1946 with our meager belongings tied into bundles. We entered a large court-yard of three- and four-story high masonry buildings surrounded by a wrought iron fence. Someone directed us to a specific building to register, receive a room assignment, and start our life as DPs, or displaced persons. I became an eleven-year-old Lithuanian DP, lucky to have all her family together in our own room.

The Hanau Displaced Persons Camp was located on Lamboy Street, and it consisted of three separate courtyards, each containing about a dozen brick or sandstone buildings. The courtyards had at least three entrance/exit gates surrounded by tall wrought iron fences. These courtyards had been a previous German Wehrmacht garrison and had a large open square in the center. The buildings had a central staircase. Facing the staircase landings were restrooms and sinks for each floor, with residential rooms running on both sides. There were probably about ten large rooms on each floor. We lived in courtyard *A* on the third floor. Since our family consisted of seven members, we had our own room. Smaller families had to share their rooms with other families or individuals, because each person was allocated so many square feet of space in order to accommodate the huge influx of refugees. To create some privacy, families divided the rooms with bed sheets or army-issue blankets.

Some buildings served special functions, such as the shower building, which was located in courtyard *C*. This courtyard contained the
main kitchen and mess rooms as well. In the back of this courtyard were
the stables, which had previously housed military horses. The courtyard had a movie theater where American movies were shown. There
was even a hospital in one of the courtyards, staffed by American and
DP professionals. An elementary school, which consisted of four grades
was located in one square, and the "gymnasium" (high school), consist-
ing of eight classes, was located in another courtyard. The schools were
staffed by DP residents who had been professional educators in their
homelands.

The total population of the Hanau DP Camp was about ten thousand: about three thousand Lithuanians, two thousand Latvians, fifteen
hundred Estonians, and about thirty-five hundred Polish and Ukranian
refugees. Initially the nationalities were all mixed up, but, over time, each
had more or less their own space.

The camps had a military oversight for security and policing. UNRRA
(United Nations Refugee Rehabilitation Association) provided the basic
organizational and humanitarian aid, which was replaced by the IRO
(International Refugee Organization). Over time, as the different nationalities were separated, they established their own governance, which par-
alleled a town government. Each building had its own leader, who was
responsible for passing on information to the building residents. He was
also responsible in assigning jobs for sanitation, maintenance, and clearing
up disputes between residents.

Moving from Holzheim to a DP camp was a big adjustment. We were
back to living in one room. Our parents divided up the room with sheets
into a sleeping area and an eating area. Military sleeping cots and several
blankets were provided for each person. We had one table, a bench, and

several chairs. The kitchen area had one small cabinet for our weekly food supply, and one hot plate for cooking.

Food was distributed on a weekly basis from a central building. All blocks were assigned specific days for food distribution. Again we stood in long lines for hours to receive our allocations such as canned ham, Spam, powdered milk, sugar, coffee, chocolate bars, sardines, tea, margarine, potatoes, jam, and bread. At one point, there was a great flour shortage in all of Germany, including the refugee camps. The shortage was so severe that for a period of time, the bread we received was baked from flour mixed with sawdust. The bread tasted awful, and, when sliced, the middle was wet and pulled like unbaked dough. But this crisis passed in time.

Residents were allotted small garden spaces close to their buildings. So we had our little garden again, and we started having fresh vegetables. Tomatoes were my favorite vegetable. I still love a tomato sandwich: rye bread with butter and sun-ripened tomato, sprinkled with salt. The fresh vegetables supplemented our monotonous diet, but fresh meat was scarce. Residents scoured the neighboring villages and farms to buy meat. No one was willing to sell either meat or eggs for money, which had become worthless after the war. Personal valuables, and especially cigarettes, were highly valued and became the unofficial monetary denomination. Cigarettes were distributed by the camp authorities, and the refugees used them to trade for food from local farmers.

Some enterprising DP bought a piglet and installed it in an empty horse stable. Other residents followed this wonderful idea. Our father had acquired a bicycle and rode to nearby villages with a backpack to see how he could improve our lives. One day, he came back with a small piglet in the backpack. We put it in a small tin washtub and kept it in our room until we could make arrangements for a space in the horse stables. In time, there were hundreds of pigs in small stalls in the horse stables. We fed them food scraps such as potato peels, spoiled vegetables, leftovers enriched with oatmeal, or whatever could be spared. It became a whole enterprise, with individuals serving as butchers, others improvised smoke huts, and others acquired equipment for making sausages. Everybody visited their pigs daily, cleaned their stalls, and rubbed their pigs' backs. They were the DPs' treasure.

All of this great undertaking was illegal for sanitary reasons and the authorities became aware of this enterprise. Inspectors raided the stables, and the pigs were confiscated. I don't know what happened to the livestock, but, in time, residents acquired piglets again and treated them as well as they could, and they treasured them like family members. After the first raids, the residents became alert to upcoming inspections, and, somehow, informers alerted the livestock holders that another raid was coming up. Pig owners scrambled to take their names down from the pig stalls, hide the pigs somewhere, and clean out the stall so there was no evidence. I don't know where or how other owners hid their pigs, but one time when we were alerted of an upcoming raid, we resorted to putting our piglet in the small washtub and hid it under one of the cots. Then we children had to take turns lying on the cot until the inspectors left our building. Luckily for us, the piglet had not yet grown much. I wonder if the inspectors were deceived, if they were lenient, or if they were bribed.

Bribery and the black market ran full speed, but the stores in town were empty. The Hanau DP camp black market operated right on Lamboy Street. We looked out of our third-floor window and saw dozens of people milling around, trading for all kinds of household goods. Watches, cameras, and radios were highly priced and valued. Alcohol was another item that was highly sought; some people ran illegal stills. The tragedy was that some wound up buying methanol or wood alcohol, which caused blindness. But these were rough times, and people did some things that are hard to justify and understand.

Since DPs had plenty of cigarettes, there were many cigarette butts lying around, and youngsters from town and camp picked them up, removed the remaining tobacco, and sold it for rolling cigarettes. There were also desperate older local residents who came looking for cigarette stubs to soothe their own tobacco cravings.

It was never boring in the Hanau DP camp, at least not for the children. Each nationality organized numerous activities for children, young people, and mature residents to keep them occupied. The Lithuanians organized their activities around national pride and hope of returning home to a free Lithuania. Rumors floated around that the Western Allies would turn against Soviet Communism and liberate the Baltic countries.

The national leaders wanted to maintain the national heritage, pride, and language. Schools were established from kindergarten through twelfth grade. In Europe, elementary or primary school consisted of four grades and then came gymnasium or high school, which consisted of classes, first through eighth. The various subjects were taught by adults who had been educators in Lithuania. Since there was no college or higher education in Hanau, some of the high-school courses were taught by university professors. Religion was also a required subject. Since the Lithuanian population was about 95 percent Catholic, only Catholic doctrine was taught during regular school hours. Protestants had their religious classes during "free time."

There were many afterschool activities. There was Scouts, boys and girls, with organized camping trips in local forests where we learned how to scrub kettles, pots, and pans with sand and water since soap was still scarce. I loved the evenings by the campfire, roasting potatoes and singing folk songs. Sport activities were popular among the young people, in particular volleyball, basketball, and soccer. Teams from our camp traveled to other DP camps for competitions. There were chess clubs, stamp-collecting clubs, choir singing, folk dancing, ballet classes, handcrafts, cooking classes, and collecting old recipes, which gave measurements in pounds and liters. The Hanau camp even produced one opera each year, but not with a full orchestra.

Scouts organized yearly camps, in which numerous DP camps participated. One year, we got to travel to the German Alps, near Hitler's "Eagle's Lair." It was in a scenic location and was my first experience hiking in real mountains. Transportation was provided by American trucks. Some other travel opportunities were down the Rhine, where we saw old Germanic and Roman castles. One other memorable trip for me was visiting huge salt mines where we wore protective headgear, slid down a salt slide, and saw stalagmites and stalactites. I don't know who financed these excursions, but they were welcome adventures in the monotony of camp life.

We were free to go into the city of Hanau, whose center had been heavily bombed, but a statue for the Brothers Grimm stood intact in the middle of the city square. This was the Grimms' hometown. Since I spoke excellent German, I often frequented the Hanau city library with my sister. We sometimes went to the German movie theater, where we got to see German movies. There were no snack stands in these theaters, and it was customary to take along a sandwich and eat it while watching movies. In summer, one of the favorite pastimes was going to the lake for a swim. It was probably several miles from camp and at the edge of a forest, but we didn't think anything of walking such distances.

Another favorite hangout, especially for boys, was the sandy pine forest, where the bombed-out bunkers stood. This intriguing place was adjacent to one of the camp's courtyards. The bunkers were camouflaged among sand dunes and the aromatic pine trees. We could still see abandoned weaponry and find live ammunition in the sand. My brother Stasys and his friend opened the shells and collected the gunpowder. They fashioned guns from wood and metal pipes, included some kind of firing mechanism, and shot them off in this pine forest. Of course, it was illegal and dangerous to do that. One time, something went wrong with their invention, and the powder exploded, burning his friend's face. Luckily, it did not injure his eyes.

The other greatly anticipated event in Hanau was the arrival of donated clothing from the United States. Our clothing from Lithuania, through all the years and travels, was pretty worn out. We were a ragtag bunch. The children had not only worn out their clothing and shoes, but had outgrown them as well. When we heard that a shipment of clothing had arrived, we waited anxiously for the distribution day. Some camp residents worked for the IRO and assisted with the sorting of clothing and shoes. They passed along what items could be expected and when the allocation would occur. Single adults and parents formed lines hours ahead of time. We children sat in the room or outside our building, awaiting these gifts. It was just like getting a Christmas gift. I still remember a pale-green woolen dress that I loved. Shoes were a problem. They never fit right, and I developed some bad bunions from ill-fitting shoes. For men and adolescent boys, clothing was less of a problem. A whole warehouse of GI boots and dyed military clothing was available. All a man or adolescent needed was a note of need for specific clothing items from the camp authorities. So my brother Stasys lucked out in this instance and got a pair of boots that fit him.

Life was not so bad. We were not hungry or cold anymore, nor did we constantly fear for our lives. But there was a constant undercurrent of anxiety about the future. Where did we belong? Where could we find some acceptance and some stability? Who determined our identity? Who determined where we could live and work? There was so much uncertainty, not just unspoken anxiety, but overt events happening in the Hanau DP camp.

Shortly after the establishment of the camp, the camp authorities knew or suspected that some Nazi collaborators and sympathizers could be trying to hide among the multinational population of the refugees. Screenings were started by the military authorities. I don't know how many, if any, were identified and expelled or transferred to different facilities to answer for their past affiliations.

The next big move to decrease the refugee multitude in Germany came after the new post-World War II borders were established. Since the refugee population was predominantly from the east—Poland, Ukraine, Russia, and the Baltic countries—the Americans, the British, the French as well as the Soviets wanted these nationals to return to their liberated homelands. But most of these refugees had fled from the Communist Soviets and were in fear for their lives, slave labor, or deportation, if they returned. They had already experienced repression, torture, confiscations, deportations, and starvation under the Communists. The Baltic population escaped forced return to their homelands because the Baltic countries given to the USSR at the Potsdam Conference were considered occupied by the USSR and not independent countries.

The Ukrainian population was not so lucky. I don't know how much advance notice they had, but one day, many American trucks appeared in the Hanau DP camp, and the Ukranians, willing and unwilling, were escorted by the military and loaded into them to be returned to help rebuild their homeland. There were many tears and there was visible fear in the faces of these victims of war. We stood by and watched this tragedy unfold, feeling relief for ourselves and pity for those unable to steer the direction of their own lives.

The question of who was a legitimate refugee and, therefore, eligible for the protection and benefits of the displaced persons camp played itself out among the Lithuanian refugees as well. Since about 95 percent of Lithuanians were Catholic, the Protestant Lithuanians were the most frequently reported as being German collaborators. A "screening commission" was established, and the suspected individuals and heads of households had to appear for screening before this commission. One deciding factor was the year they left Lithuania. Some nationalistic individuals wanted to expel all Lithuanians who had left Lithuania in 1941 during the "Non-Aggression Pact" between Nazi Germany and Soviet Russia. Documents and testimonials had to be presented to clear one's family. Our family had to go before the screening commission. This was a cruel reminder of all the interrogations our mother had to go through by the Nazi authorities. At some point, this commission was dissolved, because not only the validity of the accusations, but also the question of legitimacy of who was, or was not, a refugee, was rather foggy.

One of the greatest adjustments for me was attending the Lithuanian school. When we arrived in Hanau, the school year had already started. Up to that point, I had attended only German schools. I could speak correct Lithuanian, but the Lithuanian language has complex grammar and writing rules. I was assigned to our first gymnasium class based on my age, which was about twelve. The first day I attended school in the Lithuanian language class, we all had to take dictation. I had a lot of trouble, but I wrote the best I could. The papers were collected at the end of the dictation and handed to the teacher. The teacher pulled my paper out and called me to the front desk to read it aloud while he corrected it. I had made one mistake on top of another, one red mark upon another. I started crying, but I had to read through the whole paper. I did get through it in spite of my tears. The teacher looked at me and said, "It looks hopeless, Miss Neimanas (my maiden name)," and then gave me the mark 1 =, the equivalent of F with 2 minuses. The classroom was completely silent. I felt humiliated and exposed as incompetent in front of all my classmates. It was like standing naked in front of everyone. I don't remember what happened during the rest of the class, nor do I remember the rest of the school day.

I don't know what I told my mother after that day, but she started tutoring me everyday after school. I do know I never worked so hard to master a subject, to redeem myself before my peers and prove my teacher wrong. I was not fighting for acceptance. I was fighting to prove my teacher's and my classmates' perceptions of me as wrong. I had been deeply hurt. I am lucky in that my mother had excellent knowledge of the Lithuanian language and its grammar rules. By the end of the first year, my Lithuanian language teacher called me "professor" and called on me when my classmates were unable to answer a question. In some ways, I felt redeemed in the eyes of my peers and my teacher, but I don't think I ever completely recovered from this experience: my own feeling of deficiency, the public exposure of my defect, and someone putting me or anyone else through such humiliation.

I don't remember how long it took for me to be accepted by my classmates, but I made friends and was well liked by most of them. I didn't have any difficulty in the other classes and excelled in some, but particularly in German, which was a required language course. It was obvious to my teacher and to my classmates that I was fluent in German. During test time, many of my classmates wanted to sit next to me so that they could kibitz and improve their grades. But my knowledge of German also marked me in this post-Nazi period. One day during recess while we were playing outside in the courtyard, a classmate came up to me and whispered, "Nazi." I stopped in the middle of whatever I was doing and physically attacked her. We wrestled on the ground, and she wound up with a bloody nose. This is the only physical fight I had with anyone.

I can't remember if I was punished by the school or not, but I wouldn't have cared. I was deeply wounded by that word, "Nazi." The girl who called me that had no idea of my experiences and feelings regarding Nazi policies. I felt betrayed. When we lived in Germany and I attended their schools, I never felt accepted, but I knew that I was a "foreigner" and did not expect anything better. But when we were admitted to the Hanau Displaced Persons Camp and were with the Lithuanians, I believed we were with our own people, where we belonged. Not all my classmates saw me as an outsider, an enemy of the true Lithuanians, but I became aware that the Lithuanians who fled from the Communists in 1941 and were Protestant and spoke German were under much greater scrutiny about where their loyalties lay.

Religion was important for the Catholics as a base for community building and was just as important for the Protestants, although we were a much smaller group. My father was the only Protestant minister in Hanau and ministered to all the Protestant denominations, not only in Hanau. He visited other DP camps that did not have their own ministers. We had weekly church services and religious education in preparation for confirmation. Baptisms were performed, as well as weddings. We had our own youth group that met regularly to socialize. There was always someone who had an accordion and played popular dance music.

It was here in Hanau that I formed lifelong friendships with three other girls, who had also left Lithuania in 1941. One of my friends was Catholic, and her family that was ousted from the DP camp because their name was "too German." Her family had to find housing outside the camp. They were not eligible for the care packages or assistance with used clothing. The only good thing was that my friend and her two brothers were permitted to attend our Lithuanian school. Years later, we reconnected in the Chicago area and have remained close friends, bound by our common past experience.

The predominant concern throughout all these events was the future. Where could we find a haven for our families, earn a living, have jobs? Where could our children have a future, find a vocation or a profession, practice their faith, and have a home with some measure of privacy? Families did not want to depend on the generosity of others and be indebted. Initially, people hoped that the Western Allies would break allegiance with the Soviet Communists and liberate the Baltic countries, but that proved to be a pipe dream. Families who had relatives in America considered themselves lucky; not only did they start receiving packages, but they also had a greater possibility of immigrating to the United States.

The immigration quota into the United States did not increase after the war. For a refugee family to immigrate to the United States, their relatives in the United States had to sponsor the family by providing proof that they had the financial resources to care for the new immigrants. My mother had two cousins in the United States, but they had lost touch with one another years earlier. Our family had to find a different immigration route.

The first country to open their doors to the refugees for immigration was Canada. But Canada only wanted single, strong males to work in their farms. The men would have to commit themselves to several years of labor and leave their families behind. After their contract time, they could pay for their family's immigration costs. This was a difficult choice to make after the dangers and hardships the families had made to stay together as a family.

England also opened its doors to single men and women to help rebuild the country. England had suffered great industrial and population losses during the war and needed manpower. Australia became the next country to welcome refugee families. However, they also had criteria for eligibility. The refugee family had to be of good health with children old enough to join the labor force. Our family applied for immigration to Australia, but our father did not pass the health requirements. Other families left Hanau, looking at a more hopeful future, but our family appeared to be stuck in the displaced persons camp.

"The Displaced Persons Act of 1948," signed by President Truman, changed the fate of a multitude of refugees living in displaced persons camps. This new law permitted war refugees to immigrate into the United States for permanent residence if they could show the immigration committee that they would be employed.

Many Lithuanians already lived in the United States since the early 1900s to avoid a twenty-five-year draft into the Russian Army. There were also a significant number of Lithuanians who had emigrated from the displaced persons camps before 1948, because their relatives had sponsored them. Some had come in a roundabout way from South America and Sweden. These recent immigrants wanted to help their countrymen come to America. They systematically approached the Lithuanians who were already settled to become sponsors to families still living in the displaced persons camps. The immigration committee required a guarantee that family members would be employed without displacing current employees.

A small Lithuanian Protestant group that had settled in Chicago found a farmer in Indiana, a Lithuanian, who was willing to sponsor our family. So we prepared ourselves for a voyage across the Atlantic to settle on a farm in Argos, Indiana.

Our father acquired some wooden boards, metal hinges, and locks. He made two large crates for storing the belongings that would go in the baggage compartment and not be accessible to us until we arrived in the United States. In anticipation of our journey, our parents did their best to get us clothing that was not threadbare. I don't know what the rest of the family members got, but I went with my mother by train to a seamstress in Frankfurt on Main. She took my measurements, and I had to return for a fitting for my "going to America" dress. I can't say I liked the dress, as the seamstress put tassels on the pockets and shoulders, which she said were "cowboy-style" decoration. There was nothing I could say to object. I didn't know any better or what was in style in America. It was also for this occasion that I went with my mother to Hanau's center, where the Grimm's Brothers statue stood. Most of the buildings were destroyed, but the rubble had been cleared off the streets, and a few shops were open. We went to a shoe store. There was not much of a selection, but I got my first pair of shoes that fit and did not pinch my toes or rub my heels. It was a great relief to wear them, and I skipped down the street.

The next step for the voyage to America was going to the screening-and-transition camp in Bad Kreuznach. We were eager to go, but brother Stasys came down with a high fever and a severe ear infection. We would not be eligible to enter this transition camp, because of fear of being contagious and infecting other travelers. We had only a limited amount of time to bring Stasys's fever and ear infection under control. Penicillin was already available but only to military personnel, not the DP camp residents. The DP camp physician, who was a Lithuanian camp resident, had to petition the military medical facility for an emergency treatment with penicillin. It took several days of worry about Stasys's health and waiting for penicillin. We were overjoyed when the camp physician came to our door with the good news and a syringe to inject the miracle drug. I don't remember how many injections Stasys got, but, in several days, he started to feel better, the temperature dropped to normal, and the ear infection cleared up. We made the deadline for Bad Kreuznach. There was hope. We were on our way to America!

Entrance gate to "Displaced Persons' Camp", in Hanau,
a former German military garrison

My parents in our room, in DP camp, where our
family of seven lived from 1946 to 1950

My father, Rev. Stasys Neimanas and Rev. Fritzas
Barnelis with the confirmation class, 1946

Family and friends celebrating confirmation of sister Rita,
brother, Stasys, and cousin, Renate in our room, 1946

My confirmation class in 1947, in "DP Camp", Hanau.

With my parents on my confirmation day, 1947

Sister, Rita's high school graduating class in front of building housing the
Lithuanian school administration, and the high school in exile, in Hanau, 1949

Sister, Rita with classmates waiting for the opening of a performance
in the cinema, in DP camp, Hanau, playing American movies

Girl Scout exhibition performance on parade grounds in DP camp, Hanau, 1947/48

Camping, for scouts was another welcome activity to break the
monotony, of living in crowded conditions, in DP camps. 1948

DP camp, Hanau, 1947: line waiting for food distribution.

DP camp, Hanau, 1946: some new refugees arrive.

One of the two trunks my father built for our voyage to Argos, Indiana, U.S.A.

Going to America

&

BAD KREUZNACH WAS NOT FAR from Hanau, and I have no recollection of how we got there. This camp was the final step for one more evaluation to show we were eligible for immigration to the United States.

Our two large wooden crates were ready with everyone's cargo luggage. We only had basic clothing and documents with us. In this camp, we had no privacy. We were sheltered in a large building like a gym, which may have been a warehouse. There were rows of army cots with military blankets and pillows. At this point, we all had large identification tags that we had to wear around our necks at all times. We ate in a large mess hall. Our parents and any other adult family members were called up for document screenings, criminal records, and previous collaboration with the Nazi regime and a valid sponsor. There were also various physical examinations for everyone waiting to emigrate. We had to receive various immunizations and tests to check for tuberculosis.

This screening/transition camp also served as a quarantine station to prevent the spread of communicable diseases. We were not allowed to leave the camp, nor was anyone allowed to visit us. We stayed in Bad Kreuznach for approximately two weeks, which are mostly a blur in my mind. I can't say that time went by fast or slow; I was just doing what we were told to do, going from one examination station to the next, repeating my name and having my identification tag checked over and over again.

Toward the end of February 1950, we were put on a train. This time, it was a passenger train that took us nonstop for our next and final stay in Germany—Bremen Hafen. This was a huge camp with a multitude of buildings. Men and adolescent boys were separated from women and children. Again our shelter was large open barracks, with one army cot next to the other, and only a few feet apart. Meals were served in large mess halls, and we had to wear our large identification tags at all times. But there was a difference, as we were able to leave the camp during the daytime and go into the town proper. There were some stores and, apparently, our parents still had some German money. They bought a wristwatch for me—my very first watch. I was so happy and felt so adult at the age of fifteen, wearing a watch. I checked the time every few minutes, just to admire my gold-colored watch with a fine leather wristband. I don't know how it happened, but on the second day, as I was wearing my visible sign of being a responsible person, I lost the watch. I was in tears, tormented by the loss. I felt guilty for being careless and wasting my parents' money. I should have enjoyed those last few days, daydreaming about the upcoming voyage and all the wonderful things I would see and experience, but all I felt was gloom and self-blame.

Bremen Hafen was one of the largest ports in Germany, and there were several ships in the harbor. There were many people waiting for departures to all over the world, not just on our ship, the *General Hershey*. *General Hershey* was a military troop transport ship being used to transport immigrants to America. So one cold, gray morning, we were herded like sheep with our tags and measly hand luggage to board for our voyage. We stood for hours, freezing, while the line moved forward at a snail's pace, up the ramp and down metal stairs, deeper and deeper into the ship. Men and boys were led into one part of the ship, and women and children into another.

We got to our assigned level, which was filled with four-tier bunk beds, with little space between the bunks and tiers. The tiers of the canvas beds did not have enough space between them to be able to sit up straight. We had to crawl into our bunks and huddle or lie down. The area was dark, with poor lighting, and the air had a damp, sour smell. Our mother, sister Rita, nanny Ane, brother Johnny, and I were assigned bunk beds across the narrow aisle. Nanny Ane and Johnny were on one side, our mother had the bottom bunk across the aisle, I was on the second tier, and sister Rita had the third tier. We stored our hand luggage on the top tier. I have no idea who was next to us, nor who occupied the tier above our nanny Ane and brother Johnny.

After we settled in as best as we could and all the passengers had boarded the *General Hershey*, the ship remained in the harbor overnight. The ship swaying gently in the waves, and some passengers already started getting seasick. This was the beginning of March, the season of storms in the Northern Atlantic. We wondered what would happen to all of us. As we set off into the ocean, the swaying of the ship increased as did the number of seasick people. Lucky for us, the ship's crew cleaned up the floors in the narrow spaces between the bunk beds. In spite of the cleaning, the sour odor increased in the berth sections. People tried to make it to the toilets, but these were few and far between, and most did not make it. It was misery.

I don't remember seeing brother Stasys or our father during the voyage. We went to the large dining rooms at different times, depending on the section of the ship where we were berthed. At times there were many diners, and many times there were few, depending on the weather conditions and the accompanying sea sickness. Our mother and nanny Ane suffered from severe sea sickness and spent most of their time in their bunks. I don't remember how they managed to take care of brother Johnny, nor do I remember who brought my mother or nanny Ane any nourishment.

I spent most of my time during the voyage with my sister, Rita. Luckily we both tolerated the swaying of the ship quite well. There were a number of storms during our voyage, when the waves were so high that the doors to the decks were locked to prevent passengers from being swept overboard. These were miserable times; more people were seasick, and the stagnant air in the bunk areas smelled even worse. There was no place to go but to lie in our bunks. We could either sleep or talk, but reading was impossible, because the light was dim.

When it was time for our passenger section to have meals, Rita and I helped in the dining area. We put salt and pepper on the table as well as bread and pitchers of water. The tables were covered with tablecloths, which I thought was elegant, but when there was greater wave action, everything slid off the tables. So when the weather was rough, a crew member poured water over the table to keep things from sliding off and creating a big mess.

It was in the dining area where I saw an African American up close. He was one of the ship's crew members and wore a white uniform. Rita and I tried to talk to him in our poor English. I think he had as difficult a time understanding us as we had understanding him. I believe he told us that he lived in a city with his parents and several brothers and sisters. He was friendly and polite. This was the first time that we tried to speak English outside of a classroom.

When weather permitted, passengers were allowed to go on deck and get some fresh air. There were several decks, and everyone who was able to get out of their bunks rushed outside. There were deck chairs, but they were always filled with adults and older passengers. Teenagers and young people would not dream of taking the deck chairs when there were older people or mothers with small children trying to get chairs.

The air temperature was above freezing, but it was quite windy, and we needed coats to be outside. There were always ropes strung along the ship to grip when waves washed unexpectedly over the deck. The seas were pretty high at times when we were on deck. I could see the oncoming wave well above our bow, as *General Hershey* slid down the preceding wave. It was thrilling, exciting, and scary; my heart was pounding. We held on tight, expecting the oncoming wave to wash over us. At times the wave washed over the bow, but at other times, the trough of the wave was wide enough for the ship to just ride up, like on a roller coaster.

In calmer weather, we stood at the railing and watched the immense sea and the waves, wondering what there was beneath us. It was always special when dolphins accompanied the ship, at times riding beside it and sometimes racing to the bow. People lined up three deep at the railing to get a glimpse of the porpoises playing in the vast sea. It lifted our spirits and our moods to see such beautiful creatures at play. Dolphins were not the only sea creatures we saw; we also saw flying fish, small creatures in comparison to the dolphins. They appeared out of relatively low waves, flying several feet above the water with stubby outstretched fins at their sides and disappearing into the oncoming waves. They appeared in bunches, like flocking birds.

We spent as much time as possible on deck, enjoying the fresh air, the ocean spraying on our faces. It was much better than being in the bunk area in dim light and stale air. Then one day an announcement was made through the intercom that we were approaching the Statue of Liberty. Everybody, including those who had spent most of the voyage in their bunks, climbed the iron stairs to get on deck to view the Statue of Liberty, the sign of freedom and opportunity, the land of our hopes.

I do not know how long we were on deck, but it seemed that soon another announcement was made. We were instructed to return to our bunks and get ready to disembark. There was not much for us to do to get ready. We tried to groom ourselves as best as we could; we washed our faces and combed our hair to be as presentable as possible. We had only a bit of hand luggage, our winter coats, and our name tags.

We heard the ship's engines change their sound and speed. We felt more sudden changes in speed, almost like bumps. It seemed like a long, long time before the ship came to a standstill. We were served dinner on the ship that evening, and then had to return to the bunks. I remember spending a restless night wondering what was going on outside, wondering why they did not let us out, wondering what sights I would see.

In the morning, on March 11, 1950, we disembarked section by section in the New York harbor. We were dressed in our winter coats and hats and stood in a slow-moving line for hours till we got to the upper deck. The sky was overcast, and it looked like another gloomy day. I saw nothing except the people in front and to the side of us. Everyone was carrying bundles, holding their children's hands, carrying babies, and looking tired. I clung close to my mother; nanny Ane, who was holding Johnny's hand; and sister Rita, who carried much of our hand luggage. Slowly, we descended the ramp and found ourselves on a huge pier.

It was a long, covered pier with tables in the center from one end to the other. Officials sat at the tables, and the cargo luggage was on one side of the tables. We were led down the other side of the tables and directed by UNRRA officials to stop at a particular table to have our documents and tags checked one more time. I believe that we were reunited with our father and brother Stasys. Next our family was led to the other side of the tables to verify our wooden crates with our worldly belongings. Apparently, while we were supposedly sleeping, the crew had unloaded everyone's cargo baggage and arranged it in some order to make sure that passengers and luggage arrived at the same destination.

The next thing I remember, our family was escorted to board a passenger train. I got a window seat and was handed a pillow. I cannot remember whether we ate or drank anything that day. I'm sure we did, but I can't remember any specifics. It was like sleepwalking, being shuffled from one place to another. It was a relief to be on a train, sitting down with a pillow to put my head on, bound for Argo, Indiana.

It was toward evening, and I remember the light being on in the train. I planned to stay awake as we rode through New York, the biggest city in the world, with wonders to see. But I must have been exhausted; I dozed off and only opened my eyes briefly to see the train rush past tall buildings, at times close to lighted windows. Then I was sound asleep, with a soft pillow for my head.

I woke up when the train stopped and looked out the window. I was astonished that we were in a large train station with many tracks and a multitude of people. I had expected Argo, Indiana, to be a small station with farm fields in sight. My parents told me to get my coat on, pick up my bundles, and follow them. All our family got off the train, and we found ourselves in a large train station. We felt pretty lost and hung together in a bunch. I wondered where we were. Nobody had told me yet. Then we saw a well-dressed man striding toward us. He embraced my father, and they greeted one another in Lithuanian. Then he greeted my mother and the rest of us and led us out of the station to his car. Oh, what a surprise; what a treat! I had never been in a car before. This was Mr. Kutra's car, our family friend from Lithuania, who had come to pick us up from the train station.

We packed into the car like sardines; after all there were seven of us plus Mr. Kutra. But it did not matter. I found out that we were actually in Chicago, and he was driving us to the Variakojis family's apartment on 59th Street, near Halsted Avenue. We were warmly received by this hospitable family, who themselves had come to America only a few years earlier and lived in a second-floor apartment.

In a little while, Dr. Vaitaitis arrived with his wife and their adorable toddler daughter; they also lived on 59ᵗʰ Street, just a few doors down. These were all friends of our parents, who had worked on our behalf to come to America. They had also arranged for us to wind up in Chicago, rather than Argo, Indiana.

After treating us to delicious roast chicken, with all the right side dishes, plenty of coffee, and filled donuts for dessert, it was decided that my father, nanny Ane, and Johnny, would sleep at Dr. Vaitaitis's apartment across the street. The rest of us would sleep on the floor in Variakojis' living room. So began our life in America. This was March 11, 1950. I was fifteen years old.

Our family was grateful that we had a roof over our heads, but we also knew that this was a great hardship and inconvenience for the Variakojis family. So after a couple days of rest, our whole family set off for the US Social Security Department. All of us had received green cards when we entered the United States. These cards, which are still in use today, allowed us permanent residence in America, a right to apply for citizenship, and a right to work. However, to work, we also needed to have Social Security cards. Somebody drove us there. Brother Stasys told me that someone who knew English better than we did accompanied us, but it was not hard to fill out the required form and present the green cards. We received our Social Security cards and were ready to take the next step to go and look for jobs.

Mr. Kutra came with his car to take us to various companies to apply for jobs. Initially he took our father, sister Rita, brother Stasys, and me. Our mother, nanny Ane, and Johnny remained at home. As I remember, our father, my brother Stasys, and I got jobs at Hart Schaffner & Marx, a men's clothing factory. Stasys's job was in the cutting room, and my job was with eight women at a table with bright overhead lights sewing button holes in suit jackets, and our father was hired as a janitor. Rita got a job at the Florsheim Shoe factory. Later my mother also started working in a furniture factory. We all handed over our earnings to our parents so the money would be used wisely, depending on our needs. It felt good that we had some income and were able to meet our essential needs.

Through the assistance of the Presbyterian Church, we got an apartment in a duplex on 71st Street and Michigan Avenue, a nice residential neighborhood. We considered ourselves lucky to have such a nice apartment because there was a housing shortage, one of the consequences of the postwar. The GIs, discharged soldiers, had returned and started their families. They wanted to resume a normal family life. There was a great influx of refugees from Europe seeking a place of stability. Many came to Chicago. There was an already established Lithuanian community, and the new arrivals felt less like strangers. Many African Americans were leaving the Southern States to resettle in Chicago and other Midwestern cities, seeking a less discriminatory environment. All of this sudden population increase created a great housing shortage.

Our apartment was on the second floor. We had a kitchen with a pantry, a bathroom with hot and cold water, a living room, and three bedrooms. It was luxurious in my eyes; we had so much space and privacy.

At the corner of the next block was a Presbyterian church, where our father held the first Lithuanian Evangelical Reformed Church service for the Lithuanian Evangelical Reformed refugees in the Lithuanian language. This congregation brought together many old friends and acquaintances who had known and helped one another in the past.

By the fall of 1950, we were familiar with the Chicago Public Transportation System and were able to get around easily and take advantage of the great museums, art galleries, and beaches and parks, which were free. Our English had improved enough that we wanted to continue our education. Sister Rita started as a freshman at the University of Illinois at Navy Pier in Chicago. She also found a night job at a letter factory so she could continue contributing financially. Brother Stasys and I enrolled in Harper High School, on 65th Street and Wood Avenue, him as a senior, and me as a junior. Brother Johnny started elementary school. Nanny Ane continued to take care of our home and all of us. We had survived the currents of wartime.

Our first family photo in America, Bridgeport neighborhood, Chicago, Illinois, 1951.

The four of "us", FREE at last! 1951.

Conclusion

$\backsim\!\!\!\!\!\sim$

LIVING IN THE UNITED STATES required many adjustments, not just a new language. We could understand written English, but it was a challenge to understand the spoken language. Initially, all the words seemed to flow together.

Many of the Lithuanian displaced persons who came to Chicago chose to live in established Lithuanian neighborhoods such as Bridgeport, Marquette Park, or Brighton Park. Initially, our family lived in Bridgeport as well, close to the stockyards. There were small stores still in business in 1950, where we could make our purchases without speaking English.

There were also new customs to learn, as, for instance, women and men did not shake hands, and girls did not curtsy when greeting adults. These differences were not greatly important but appeared strange initially. We had to learn new manners by watching how others behaved, watching movies, or being corrected by others. The trick was to remember what manners to use when in company of Americans and when in company of older Lithuanians who were recent arrivals from Europe. Most Americans were quite accepting of our eccentricities or peculiar manners. The Europeans were more formal and demanding in their expectations of proper behavior. Europeans never addressed adults by their first names unless they were close friends or relatives. We never sat down in a bus or train if an older person was present. Another example was when a teacher entered the classroom, all students rose and stood until permitted to sit.

My parents were proud of our heritage and my father and sister Rita continued to participate in the Lithuanian cultural and social events. Nevertheless they chose to move to a community that was well integrated. As soon as my parents saved up for a down payment on a modest home, they moved to Evanston, Illinois, where they lived to the end of their lives with sister Rita.

As we became more integrated and settled, I had more time to think about how different life was in America and wonder about how our experiences of the war years had changed me. We did not talk about it in our family; it was a taboo. If we talked about these events, we asked specific questions to verify facts. I believe it was too painful for my parents to think or talk about those years, when we were carried by the currents of war.

When I think about those nine turbulent years, I realize how difficult it must have been for my parents to raise us in a world where they had almost no control of their own or their children's lives. They abhorred the cruelty and intolerance they saw and experienced in Nazi Germany, not just against us, but particularly against Jewish, Russian, and Polish people. They saw how Nazi Germany used the church to try to indoctrinate intolerance and hatred against anyone who disagreed with their doctrine. How, in spite of all the intolerance and threats, did my parents teach us to be respectful of other cultures, religions, and human beings?

Throughout the years, I wonder what impact those nine years of unsettled life had on our family and how they shaped my personality and my values. I don't think I would understand and appreciate the power of hunger and starvation if I had not lived in Nazi Germany and witnessed the fight for a half slice of bread. I am grateful that although our family had to forage and scavenge, we never experienced the degree of hunger that many less fortunate experienced and even died from starvation.

I don't remember knowing the word "prejudice" in my childhood, although it existed on so many levels in so many places. It seems to me that there is no country that is free of some type of prejudice. Although I did not know the word "prejudice," I got to experience it and learn about it during those turbulent years in Europe. It is a biting and bitter experience against which it is hard to defend oneself. There is nothing rational about it, but the underlying message behind it is, "You are worthless"; "I am better than you." I found it particularly painful and infuriating when I did not expect to be the recipient of degrading, stigmatizing remarks.

I remember two clear instances. We were returning to Lithuania, and the whole boxcar fell silent because I uttered one simple word, *"Mutti"*. Mommy. The other instance was when we lived in Hanau, the displaced peoples' camp, and a classmate whispered to me, "Nazi."

But I also found that there are kind and courageous people who will extend helping hands, even at risk to themselves. I am grateful that our family managed to somehow stay together. Our shared experiences brought us closer together and made us more appreciative of one another. We never lost touch with our extended family who are scattered over several continents. We enjoy getting together and feel kinship. Family loyalty and helping those who are less fortunate are highly valued by all our family members.

I don't know in what ways my life and I would have been different if World War II had not happened. It was a difficult time, but I am glad for many experiences I had. I got to meet people of many nationalities and a multitude of customs. I learned several languages and heard many more. I found that most people want to have decent lives, raise their families, and do something meaningful in life. I also learned that fear, prejudice, and scarcity of resources can cause people to act in cruel, brutal, and unfair ways.

I am grateful that John Kiaulinas, from Argos, Indiana, was willing to be our sponsor so that we could come to the United States, although he did not know us at all. Our father met him at a Lithuanian gathering in Baltimore several years after we had come to America. My father thanked him for being willing to take a chance on our family and give us an opportunity of a decent life. It is only recently that my brother Stasys and his wife, Margret, visited Argos, Indiana, where Mr. Kiaulinas is buried, to show our appreciation for his trust and belief in us, who were strangers to him.

Places Where I Lived, Carried by the Currents of War

1. Nemunelio-Radviliskis, Lithuania: my parents' home
2. Utrata, Poland: a screening/transition camp
3. Teodoris, East Prussia: a second screening camp
4. Wangerin, Pommern (Wogorzyno, Poland): a camp for foreigners—an "A" Lager
5. Koeslin, Pommern (Koszalin, Poland): a camp for "Germanized" Foreigners—an "O" Lager
6. Papilys, occupied Lithuania: my father's childhood hometown
7. Koelln, Prussia: an abandoned homestead
8. Koellner Huette, Prussia: an abandoned school
9. Holzheim, Germany
10. Hanau, Germany: a DP camp
11. Chicago, Illinois

Acknowledgments

⟋ᴄ⟍

I AM GRATEFUL TO MANY family members and friends, who at family gatherings or casual conversations heard us talking about our life and experiences of those nine turbulent war years. They encouraged me to write it down for future generations. It took me more than fifty years to get started to undertake this immense task.

I thank my sister-in-law Margaret Neimanas, for being the reader of the first pages of the family story and encouraging me to continue. My friend Linda Richman, encouraged me from the very beginning to the end of this undertaking to keep going. Her interest in the holocaust and events in East Europe during the war years led to many discussions and consolidated my thoughts.

My brother Stasys, confirmed some of my recollections that I was not quite sure about and added recollections from his experience. My cousin, Renate, contributed in various ways. She has an excellent memory for names of places and the emotional tone of events. It is Renate, who gave me the copy of Onyte Ycas letter written in 1941, as well as the drawings by Onyte Ycas of our trek by covered wagon as we were fleeing from Lithuania, in 1944.

As my manuscript grew, I asked my friend and former colleague Christine Bruun, to read and edit my story. In spite of her very busy schedule she spent hours reading and editing.

I am also grateful to Connie Fetzer for reading, editing, and encouraging me to keep going. I wanted Connie's feedback, because I saw her as an impartial but sensitive reader. I still need reassurance at times.

My grandson Nicholas Lancaster and my friend Cathy Moats assisted me in dealing with the computer, which is still a challenge. I have not mastered the computer's language yet and need help. I appreciate the time they spent and their patience responding to my basic questions.

My son Markus and Susan were a consistent support for me from beginning to end of this project.